MARILYN

HANNAH, GET UP

I AM HANNAH

BASED ON A TRUE-LIFE JOURNEY

FOREWORD BY: DICKERSON L. S. WELLS, DMIN

TRILOGY
A WHOLLY OWNED SUBSIDIARY OF **TBN**
PROFESSIONAL PUBLISHING MEETS POWERFUL PROMOTION

Trilogy Christian Publishers
A Wholly Owned Subsidiary of Trinity Broadcasting Network
2442 Michelle Drive
Tustin, CA 92780
Copyright © 2024 by Marilyn Y. Murphy
Scripture quotations marked GW are taken from GOD'S WORD®, © 1995 God's Word to the Nations. Used by permission of God's Word Mission Society.
Scripture quotations marked KJV are taken from The Holy Bible, King James Version. Cambridge Edition: 1769.
Scripture quotations marked NIV are taken from THE HOLY BIBLE, NEW INTERNATIONAL VERSION®, NIV® Copyright © 1973, 1978, 1984, 2011 by Biblica, Inc.® Used by permission. All rights reserved worldwide.

Scripture quotations marked NLT are taken from the Holy Bible, New Living Translation, copyright © 1996, 2004, 2015 by Tyndale House Foundation. Used by permission of Tyndale House Publishers, Inc., Carol Stream, Illinois 60188. All rights reserved.
Scripture quotations marked NKJV are taken from the New King James Version®. Copyright © 1982 by Thomas Nelson. Used by permission. All rights reserved.
All rights reserved, including the right to reproduce this book or portions thereof in any form whatsoever.
For information, address Trilogy Christian Publishing
Rights Department, 2442 Michelle Drive, Tustin, CA 92780.
Trilogy Christian Publishing/ TBN and colophon are trademarks of Trinity Broadcasting Network.
For information about special discounts for bulk purchases, please contact Trilogy Christian Publishing.
Trilogy Disclaimer: The views and content expressed in this book are those of the author and may not necessarily reflect the views and doctrine of Trilogy Christian Publishing or the Trinity Broadcasting Network.

10 9 8 7 6 5 4 3 2 1
Library of Congress Cataloging-in-Publication Data is available.
ISBN 979-8-89333-719-8
ISBN (ebook) 979-8-89333-720-4

DEDICATION

I dedicate this book to everyone in my world who has
shaped me into becoming who I am today,
from day one until now.

I especially want to say thank you to
my loving husband, children, parents, and our siblings,
whose endless love and support makes me
feel like I can achieve anything.

To Julia Hale, Brenda Houston, Arella Adams,
Joyce Adams, and Diane Keesee:
Thank you for being there.
You all were God-sent to assist me when I needed it most.

To Lenora McLean, my aunt and English
teacher who is now 93 years old.
I pray that my words make you proud. I love you.

To Mother Daisy Houston who prophesied years ago,
"I see you writing a book." Thank you;
it pushed me to keep going.

To my goddaughter, Joylika Adams, thank you for the
letter and hand writing the poem. It brought
me such comfort, and yes, I still have it.

SPECIAL DEDICATION

In loving memory of Elder Grady Henderson, Jr.,
who saw me in the spirit way before I did.
I'm thankful to him for speaking life into me.
I heard him and held his words close.
The memory of his big smile lingers on.

Finally, to our little lady, Mariah Yvette Murphy,
our stillborn baby, you are my inspiration.
Your purpose has been fulfilled.

FOREWORD

Hannah, Get Up: I Am Hannah is a profound and heartfelt story of how Marilyn Murphy, her husband Erskine, and daughter Kristyn emerged from a period of deep consternation to a peak of joy and victory. As you journey with Marilyn through the pages of this book, you will learn not only of a woman and her family who faced problems, but how they stood up and conquered them with prayer, faith, and praise.

Marilyn reveals that a prayer life confesses our inability to deal with the crisis at hand and how prayer causes us to admit that without God we can do nothing. She further points out that faithfulness is what God always requires of us no matter what we face in life, and how faith does not make light of our present realities, but simply acknowledges that all things are possible with God. Finally, the author helps the reader to understand how important it is to have the kind of faith that can praise God as you go through, for it is the praise that we give unto the Lord that gives us new strength to continue and face each day.

It is my hope that you too will learn the secret of how Hannah stood and moved from dismay and confusion to joy and victory and then apply it to your life.

Dickerson L. S. Wells, DMin

TABLE OF CONTENTS

Dedication 5

Special Dedication 7

Foreword 9

Letter from the Author 13

Introduction 17

Chapter One: Two Hannahs 23

Chapter Two: Suffering in Silence 41

Chapter Three: Where Do We Go from Here? 47

Chapter Four: Drown Out the Noise 63

Chapter Five: Into the Position of Seek 73

Chapter Six: Keep the House Strong 87

Chapter Seven: God, YOU Promised a Wealthy Place . . 101

Chapter Eight: A New Beginning 113

Chapter Nine: Hannah, Get Up 121

Chapter Ten: You Were in My Path 133

Endnotes 141

LETTER FROM THE AUTHOR

Dear Reader,

Whether male or female, after reading this book, I pray that you would have found yourself somewhere in its pages as this book has been lived out, prayed out, and birthed out. I always desired to write a book. After much time in prayer, I heard the Spirit of the Lord say, "It's time."

It is my prayer that you receive encouragement from it as you go through your own life journey. Remember, you've got this. Whether you know it or not, my journey with you doesn't stop after you finish reading this book. It started before you decided to pick it up. Paul said in Ephesians 1:16 NIV, "I have not stopped giving thanks for you, remembering you in my prayers." I, like Paul, have a special place in my heart for those who connect with me. It is my prayer that the Lord blesses you, the reader of this book, overwhelmingly. I may not know you personally, but that does not matter. I pray this book gives you what you need to get up and keep moving in the direction of God.

My friend, your journey may get so hard that you will not feel like going on. Trust me! I understand. I've been there. But I speak to you by the power and authority of the Holy Spirit that you shall live and not die. You can get through whatever you are facing. Keep the phrase "Our trials come to make us stronger" in the forefront of your mind. Use it as a motivator. Let it drive you. From the hills and valleys that I have experienced in my lifetime, I can truly say that I have been made stronger because of them. Things that used to bother me no longer affect me. I've even whispered the prayer, like Jesus in Luke 23:34 KJV, "Father, forgive them, for they know not what they do."

I have learned that with anything we go through, we must be on guard. For our adversary, the devil, looks for anything that will discourage, hinder, and overthrow the plans of God for our lives. When we are in the midst of a trial, we must remember that we serve the Omnipotent, All-Powerful God. We must stay on guard and on point to use our weapons to defeat any form of giant that comes our way. They do not have the upper hand. We do! They have not been guaranteed the victory. We have! With God on our side, we win! Remember that.

I prophesy that you shall live and not die. I prophesy that you will live out your full God-intended days. I prophesy that you will believe in the Lord Jesus Christ and Him crucified and that you will walk after the Spirit[1] as Paul advised us in Romans. I prophesy that you will come through your trials like a champion that has been fortified by the power of the Holy Spirit.

Remember that Romans 8:35-37 KJV encourages us and calls us more than conquerors. Despite troubles, sufferings, persecutions, lack, neediness, danger, and even in the face of death, we have victory through Christ. I love how the New Living Translation describes it as not only a victory, but an overwhelming victory. That means it's no contest. We win by a landslide, with no chance of losing. It's breathtaking. It is an absolute, complete, overcoming, and guaranteed victory.

This is why you can move forward. All you have to do is make up your mind that no one, no tactic, no snare, no disguise, no weapon, no distraction, no trap, no wicked device, no scheme, no plot, no plan, no hinderance, or any such thing will keep you from getting up and on with what God has called you to be and do.

The choice is ultimately yours. However, I highly suggest that you make up your mind that you want all that God has for you. God's Word is there to instruct and guide you through the entire journey and His Spirit is there with you now, to dwell on the inside of you. Your next move is to pick up only what needs to go with you and leave alone what or who needs to be left behind. Move on.

Remember, this is your destiny. This is your call. This is your life. Walk it out with your head up and watch how God leads you into a path of righteousness for His name's sake that will blow your mind.

I'm excited for you. Enjoy the journey.

Marilyn

INTRODUCTION

Join me, if you will. Let us embark on a journey about the lives of two Hannahs, two women whose paths took unexpected turns. Things didn't quite go as planned, but who said that it was their plan in the first place? Jeremiah 29:11 NIV plainly states, "For I know the plans I have for you, declares the Lord, plans to prosper you and not to harm you, plans to give you hope and a future."

Most little girls and boys dream of the days when they will be grown and happily married with children. All their boxes are checked, degree(s), dream job, nice home, nice car, financially stable, good friends, etc. It's the "American Dream." However, they never factor in the ups and downs, the twists and turns that life has a way of throwing in without warning. I remember asking, "Why didn't someone tell me about this?" I didn't get the memo until it happened. Then, different women of different ages and backgrounds began to talk and speak up. I heard, "It happened to me." "It happened to me too." "Oh, it happened to me as well." "Me too." Yeah, I had "Me Too" moments of my own way before America had hers. Yes, they spoke up but only after I had to stand up and join in and declare those same exact words, "ME TOO!" However, I will not be silent. Hear me, my friends. Hear me, my brothers and sisters. Hear what the Spirit is saying to you through me throughout these pages.

In the Book of 1 Samuel Chapters 1 and 2, we read the story of a woman named Hannah. Hannah, whose name means "grace and favor," found herself submerged in mental and emotional battles that would either make her or break her. I am sure many have read her story and found that they could identify with her in one way or another.

In the eyes of many women in today's society, Hannah is considered a blessed woman. To have a man adore them and spoil them like Hannah's husband treated her is very much coveted these days. However, in Hannah's day, she felt and was in the eyes of others painstakingly far from blessed. She felt desolate, in a dry place, unproductive and unfruitful. I can even imagine her being ashamed and embarrassed and she had every right to be. In her time, a woman in her state was considered cursed or as being punished by God (Varsity Company International, 1997).[1] This wasn't about how well she could cook. It wasn't about how well she could run her household. The people could care less about her social status. If you were in this state, you were considered unprivileged. You were frowned upon.

The state that Hannah found herself in brought forth such an emptiness in her. She wanted this emptiness to be filled so much until it became her greatest desire. That desire was so strong and the enemy, her enemies, knew it and tormented her simply because she did not have it.

Hannah was dealing with two enemies. She had to contend

with not only a physical enemy that was in close proximity to her but an even closer enemy, the enemy of her mind. You know, the one that tells you that you do not deserve what you desire. The one that tells you something is wrong with you and that you deserve this fate and more or even worse, the one that tells you that because this has happened, God does not love you. Yes, her enemies used that thing that she so desired and they tried to destroy her purpose, her destiny, and her life.

Then, there is the other Hannah. It is no mystery or secret. The other Hannah is me. I ask that you join me as I allow you to take a glimpse into my life. Like Hannah in the Bible, I am also blessed. I am also very much loved by my husband, and some would even say very spoiled. However, there was a time when I felt far from blessed. The enemy tried to destroy my purpose, my destiny, and my life too. But God!!!

So, buckle up and join me in the coming pages on a journey of two Hannahs. We will discover how getting into the right posture and position moved them both from being troubled into triumphant.

Enjoy the journey!

PROPHECY RECEIVED

The Lord said, "You are Hannah."

When this prophecy was received from Evangelist Bessie Mathis, I had no clue what she was talking about until the Lord gave me the message titled, "Hannah, Get Up" while in prayer in 2018. The first time I gave the message, it was in its infant stage. I was just trying to speak a Word from the Lord over the church to encourage them to move on regardless of what they were facing in their lives. The Lord was speaking, "Get Up!" I then revisited the message again in 2021 where I was invited via Zoom for one church and then in person at another church to encourage God's people. That year, in the midst of a pandemic, I spoke to three different churches giving that same message with some changes to fit the season of that congregation as the Spirit of the Lord led. It was that year, in 2021, that the Lord revealed that this message needed to be birthed into a book. It was time to encourage the masses. So, here it begins...

CHAPTER ONE

TWO HANNAHS

Reading Hannah's story in the Bible, I immediately saw a story of hurt, anguish, worry, melancholy, and hopelessness. Hannah was childless and barren. The Lord had shut up her womb so she could not have children. Her adversary, her enemy, was Peninnah, her husband's other wife. It is believed that Hannah was the first wife to Elkanah. In those days, their culture was that when the wife couldn't have children, the husband had the option to take a second wife to keep his bloodline going. So, Hannah had to not only deal with being barren, she also had to deal with, in her mind, being replaced. She was the one that was supposed to keep the bloodline going. She was the one that wanted to bless her husband with children, and it caused her so much grief. I can imagine her thinking, why couldn't he wait on God to bless us with children? Why did he have to marry someone else if he loved me so much?

Thankfully, with Hannah, her love for her husband and desire to give him children greatly outweighed what his second wife, her enemy, could do to her. Although in despair, Hannah remained steadfast and committed.

Some may ask, how can a woman so well taken care of by her husband be in such misery, hopelessness, and anguish? After all, she had it made. She had her husband's heart. He expressed to her that just having her by his side was enough. He said, in 1 Samuel 1:8 KJV, "...am not I better to thee than ten sons?" He did not require more because he loved and adored her. Hannah knew all of this, but she was at the point where words of comfort, even from the one she loved and who loved her, were not enough. She wanted to do what she was created to do. She did not want to be seen as cursed or looked down upon as if she had sinned. Her heart was pure before the Lord, and she wanted to have what the other women had. She wanted to feel complete. She wanted to be a mother, and not just a mother of someone else's children. She wanted the experience of giving birth to her own children.

As I dove deeper into understanding the life of this family, I started with the husband. Elkanah was a religious man, and he raised his family in a godly way. Yearly, they would journey to Shiloh to worship the Lord. The story points to one year in particular. The family would once again journey to Shiloh. It was in this place where they were to unify in worship and thank God for His many blessings. Worship was meant for the entire family, but Peninnah's focus was far from worship. Instead of thanking God for another year and for all His many blessings, for healthy children and a husband that provides, she allowed the devil to use her.

You see, it was a yearly thing for her to torture Hannah and remind her that she had no children. She took pleasure in bullying her. She took pleasure in seeing her low. To me, it was like she was saying, "I am the head and you are the tail. I am above and you are beneath. Look at my sons! Look at my daughters! They look like their daddy, don't they? Hey, Hannah, where are your children?"

The harassment continued yearly. So, what was really going on with Peninnah? What made her go after Hannah the way she did? I believe she wanted Elkanah to feel for her like he felt for Hannah. She didn't want to be just the baby producer. She wanted Hannah's position. Most bullies are full of jealousy and low self-esteem themselves, desiring what their victim has. Peninnah was trying to take more than lunch money from Hannah; she wanted to be who she was.

Personally, I think Hannah should have told her husband of the torture she was experiencing from Peninnah, but she suffered in silence and from what I could tell, she suffered alone, expressing her agony to no one. She was just full of sorrow, crying and unable to eat. Her husband tried to console her, but he couldn't lift her spirits. Bullying is such an evil tactic. Many people use it to make themselves feel bigger and better. They attack their prey where they are most vulnerable. Most times, those getting bullied do not tell what they are going through for fear of it getting worse. All the while it steals, kills, and destroys its victim's spirit. It leads to depression and low self-esteem, or even worse, suicide. Is this what Peninnah wanted? With Hannah out of the way, she would be first, but would she? This journey called life has a way of making us reap what we sow. The Word of God tells us that. The scripts that we write for ourselves have a way of being rewritten without our consent. However, Peninnah never took that into consideration. It was full speed ahead. She continued her intimidation against the woman I would like to call Hannah One.

Hannah One was in great despair. She needed help. She was broken and desperate for deliverance.

Now, Hannah Two's, aka Marilyn's, story starts off a little different. Just as God had promised when I accepted Him as my Lord and Savior, He sent me a husband, a man that loved the Lord and that loved me. We were in no hurry to have children. We both worked. Okay, well, me on occasion and we both went to school trying to build a better life for ourselves. We were also faithful to God.

Well, about two years into our marriage, I remember having a few sisters from the church over to our home for prayer. This was one of those times when I wasn't working (on occasion – LOL!). One of the sisters, Missionary Brenda Houston, came and prayed for me. She laid hands on my stomach and began to weep. I didn't understand what was happening at the time. She said that she didn't understand it at the time either. Little did we know that God was preparing me for one of the worst trials of my life.

It soon happened. I was with child. I remember telling my husband. He asked, "Are you happy?"

I responded, "Yes!" It was a normal pregnancy. Time soon revealed, "It's a girl." Things were going well with the pregnancy. She was a lively little one. I experienced many kicks. She was a Pentecostal baby in the making. When the music played at church and the people were rejoicing, she would rejoice too. She would kick and move as if she was leaping in my belly like John the Baptist did in Elizabeth's womb. This made me so happy. I was so excited to meet her. We had already bonded. It was just a matter of time. Our family was growing and we were ready for her arrival.

I was almost 36 weeks pregnant. The time to give birth was nearing. The nursery was ready. The diaper bag was packed. The nesting had occurred. We were ready. We were just waiting on time. It was December 31, 1996. I remember going to the watch meeting service that night. At the end of the service, my pastor called everyone up to altar. I believe he saw death. He admonished everyone to come forth to let him lay hands on them. There was no line. He said just come. So, we just jammed the front of the church to let him anoint our heads. He laid hands on everyone in the church, including me. I can only imagine what God revealed to him when he touched me. Perhaps he already knew and just used wisdom by calling everyone up so I would not be afraid of what my husband and I were about to face. Looking back, he never said anything to me, but that was the type of servant he was. They called him the "Silent Giant," and I believe God used him that night to pray for my strength. I was going to need it.

The next morning, it was New Year's Day. I noticed she wasn't kicking and moving like she normally would. I tried different tactics. I remember eating chocolate. Something sweet would always get her juices flowing and moving around, but still there was no movement. I can't remember if I said anything to anyone. I was still trying to get her to move. At this time, I wasn't thinking of getting checked out. I was just doing things to get her to kick. The next morning, January 2nd, I got up. I kept trying to get her to move. I was praying and hoping she was just inactive. I told my husband that I was going to call the doctor. I called. The doctor on call was alarmed and said, "Get to the hospital now." I knew then that my baby was gone. I began to cry as I got dressed. I still remember those moments. It was something I didn't want to face, but I had to go through it. As my husband and I were on our way to the hospital, he started to drive fast. I told him to slow down. I knew it was too late. I believe he did too. She was gone. I remember the song titled "Second Chance"[1] that was playing on the radio . God was ministering to me then with that song. Although I could hear it, I couldn't hear it. However, He planted and embedded it into my heart. I hear that song in my head even while I type these words with tears streaming down my face.

We made it to the hospital. They admitted me. They were hopeful. Trying to encourage me, but the sonogram told the true story. There my sweet baby was lifeless. I still have the image of her etched in my mind. This is why the Holy Spirit used the sister from my church to pray for me. This is why she was weeping. He knew I would need the strength to make it through this new season that was upon me. Sorrow was my meat. I didn't ask for this. I wanted to send this news back. This is not what I had planned for, but the verdict was rendered. There was no turning back from it. God had spoken. Then, to top that, they said they wanted me to go through the childbirth process. Wait! What? You want me to go through everything as if my baby is alive? At that point, it was about what was best for me. The doctor told me it would be better for my body to have her naturally versus a Cesarean section. So, I had to endure even more torture.

So, they put me in labor and I had to wait it out. It was a long process. I wanted God to work a miracle. I wanted her to live. I had to experience everything like it was a normal birth. I wanted to get it over with, but she was my first child, and it took hours.

As I think back, guess what was going on at my church, a three-day shut-in. Every year, my pastor, Elder Lonnie M. Haley, would start the year off with a shut-in on January

2nd. This year was no different and I thank God it wasn't. This was our yearly gathering, like Elkanah and his family going to Shiloh. The saints were at the church praying and I KNOW they were praying for me. God knows I needed it.

As I continue to look back, I wonder what was happening with both our moms and dads. I wonder what my brothers were thinking, and his sisters. I wonder what was going on in the minds of my nieces and nephews. I wonder how my friends and church family saw things from their perspectives. I never thought about how it affected those around me until now. However, the writing of this book revealed that they were just as invested. They were just as hurt. They were just as destroyed as my husband and I were.

As I lay there in that bed waiting, I remember one specific time looking at my husband sitting in the chair across the room, reading the newspaper. I remember thinking how easy this was for him. However, as the years have passed, I fully understand that he was destroyed just as much as I was. That paper helped him settle his mind. He knew that I would need him more than ever. I just didn't see it at the time. All I saw was the devastating news that was before me.

The wait continued. It went on all day. Labor pains were coming as they should and then there was the epidural to help me through it. Eight hours or so later, I had dilated ten centimeters and was ready to push. The doctor was saying,

"Push." Three pushes and finally, she was here, but there was no kick, no cry, no life. The life of my Pentecostal baby was no more. There was no laughter from the doctor and nurses. There was no slap to get her to cry. There was silence, just silence. They took her and did whatever they needed to do. I am sure the nurses tried to comfort me, but I can't remember it. I only remember the silence of death. Even if there was plenty of noise, I heard nothing in those first few moments. My baby was gone. Several were there, I suppose waiting. I remember several people were in the room when it was time to see her. I just don't remember who. They passed her around getting their chance to hold her. I held her too, but it was temporal. I examined her. She had ten fingers and ten toes. She was beautiful. I remember her little hand on my finger. I am so glad I got to see her. I am so glad I got to hold her. I have that memory locked in my mind. Then, they took her away and I saw her no more. Oh, the despair! Oh, the weeping! Oh, the sorrow! I wanted my baby. The little one I so wanted to meet was gone. Lord, have mercy. Oh, God. Why?!

I stayed in the hospital overnight. I remember them preparing the program for a graveside service. They asked if I wanted to have something to say. So, from the hospital bed, these are the words that became her poem...

In Loving Memory of

Miss Mariah Yvette Murphy

I carried you, my little angel, for nine long months.

I felt your pain.

My love for you, my heart did gain.

I felt your kicks and your turns.

For your love, my heart did yearn.

Your very existence gave me peace

But God saw fit for it to cease.

My God knows best. He is in charge.

Rest in His bosom, my little joy. You will always be in my heart.

You've gone away,

In Heaven to stay.

Daddy and Mommy will see you again one day.

Written by: Marilyn Murphy

Minnie Adams

We left the hospital and went to my parents' home for a couple of weeks. The family arranged for a graveside service which I was not allowed to attend. The day of her burial was upon us. I wanted to be there so badly, but there were strict rules about getting out after having a baby. That was not allowed. After twenty-five years, I finally spoke to my mom about it, asking her why she wouldn't let me go. She said that she was trying to protect me. She understood the pain that I felt. She understood the torture I had faced and would have to face. She had gone through it herself. Even though it was for her baby boy after me, her seventh pregnancy, she still hurt so bad and she wanted to shield me from all that she could. Wow! I had carried that hurt for all these many years to only find out that it wasn't just because of a strict rule. It was because she wanted to make what I had to go through easier. Selah!

So, needless to say, I didn't get the closure that I wanted and needed. I had to imagine it in my mind. The pain was surreal. I heard one of my brothers say that the funeral car had just passed by on the highway. All I could do was go into the spirit realm and pray. It hurt so bad. They told me that I prayed so loud that they could hear me outside at the basketball court, which was several feet away. I prayed until I was out of myself and was taken into a vision. There, I saw my baby. She was in all white, but she was not dead. She was alive like an angel. I saw her tumbling and rolling over on clouds as if she was playing. The Lord showed me that she was all right. She looked like she was about three years old. She was beautiful. I later found out that my sweet sister-in-law, Joyce, had purchased her a beautiful white dress to adorn her in her little casket.

We named her Mariah. That name means "God is my teacher." That name was given to her way before this happened. God truly became her teacher and through this, He would become our teacher too.

Several people came to visit the day of the service. Later that evening, a storm came through and knocked the power out. I heard one elderly lady say that she had never seen a day of a funeral that when a saint of God was laid to rest and it didn't rain. Well, Mariah was no exception. However, I really feel that the outpouring of rain was a sign to my husband and me that God would send a rain of restoration, renewal, revival, and refreshing to both of us.

Hosea 6:1-3 NLT states, "Come, let us return to the Lord. He has torn us to pieces; now He will heal us. He has injured us; now He will bandage our wounds. In just a short time He will restore us, so that we may live in His Presence. Oh, that we might know the Lord! Let us press on to know Him. He will respond to us as surely as the arrival of dawn or the coming of rains in early spring." Oh, what a beautiful passage of scripture. The rain from that storm was to me a sign that we would get through this and be triumphant. It was a sign of the dawn of our new day. Our joy was coming. It was just a matter of time.

The months ahead were hard, so very hard. All I wanted was my baby. A lady was pregnant at my church during the same time. She delivered her baby some days before I delivered mine. Upon our return to church, she walked into the church with her baby in her carrier. I remember it so plainly. We were in the Women's Sunday School class. The struggle was real. I wanted her baby as my own. It became a battle of the mind. I knew her baby girl wasn't mine, but the enemy was trying to take my mind and say that she was. But I thank God for stored-up prayers. I also thank God for the saints around me, for I am convinced that the Holy Spirit had revealed to at least one of them my struggle that day. These were the women who had taught me how to pray. These were the women that had worked the altar calls and many were saved and filled the with the Holy Spirit. So, I know that somebody was praying for me that very day at that very time. I am so thankful for knowing God as my Lord and Savior. I thank God for having a personal relationship with Him. He gave me victory that day. He fought for me. The angels of the Lord were encamped around ME. The battle changed from the desire to have her baby to just crying within, suffering in silence and praying that the Lord would give me another baby that would live.

The days continued to pass. I wasn't okay. I couldn't walk in the baby section of any store. I had closed the door to the nursery and left everything as it was. Every now and then I would go in there and look at things and touch her belongings. I would turn on her little music box. The back of the music box displayed the song's name – "Everything Is Beautiful,"[2] I didn't know the lyrics. So, I had made up my own lyrics and when I was pregnant, I would sing to Mariah. My lyrics were "Everything is beautiful. Everything is so beautiful. Everything is beautiful. Everything is wonderful." However, in all actuality, at that point in time, it was not wonderful. I was not okay, but God saw me where I was and He was helping me to see that despite all I had been through, everything was beautiful and wonderful. Romans 8:28 KJV, "And we know that all things work together for good to those who love God, to those who are the called according to His purpose."

He met me at the point of my need. He saw me in a pit like Joseph[3] in the Book of Genesis that was given the coat of many colors by his father. He saw that, like Joseph, I needed to go on a journey to get to where He was trying to take me. Understand that Joseph's coat meant favor with his natural father, but more than that. I believe that coat represented his spiritual coat and it prophesied his future. Regardless of how his brothers tried to destroy his future in the natural world, they could not destroy it spiritually.

My coat was on too. I heard the Lord speak to me years ago and say, "I want to give you every part." I took that to mean that He wanted me to experience everything about Him and to start, He was going to give me a Job experience that would turn into double for my trouble, but I had to get there. Mentally, I was still in a mode of desolation and gloom, but down on the inside I knew Jesus was going to take away that gloom and allow me to laugh again.

My doctor asked if he needed to prescribe antidepression meds to help me. I said, "No, I'm fine." One thing was for sure, God was still God to me. Even when I was in some of my roughest moments, my hope was still in Him. I just needed to get in position to pray for another child. I was Hannah. I needed help from the One, the Great I Am, that could fix my issue. I needed deliverance, and this deliverance had to come through prayer and worship. My deliverer was my God.

LET'S PRAY A PERSONAL PRAYER:

Father, here I am standing in need of You. Lord, it feels like the worst thing that could have ever happened to me has happened. It feels like things can't get any worse but somehow, they do. Lord, I feel helpless and hopeless, but still somehow, Father, something on the inside of me says keep trusting, keep believing, keep pushing. I know it is You. I know it is the Holy Spirit. Even though it seems like my back is against the wall, I know You are with me where I am.

Oh, dear Father, I have done all I know to do. I'm depleted. It feels like I have nothing else, yet in my darkest days, I hear a Yes Lord, I surrender to You." Oh God, thank You for the yes. It feels good to have the yes. That yes has given me the strength that I need. So, I push forward in You. I run to You with my Yes. I run into Your loving arms. You are my help. I reveal to You my weaknesses. I show You my vulnerabilities. You are my refuge. I yet declare it. You are my source. I yet declare it. You are my peace. Oh, I yet declare it. In this experience, although hard, I yet declare that I trust You. Your Word is embedded in me. I yet declare that I won't go back! I won't throw in the towel! I will continue on this journey. I will see the goodness of God. I will continue to hope in my God, for I yet have hope because I yet have my Yes! Thank You for the Yes!

It is in Jesus' Name that I pray. Amen.

PROPHECY RECEIVED

"The Lord is going to send you a husband."

It was a Friday night. I had come home for the weekend from college. My boyfriend and I had planned a date night, but my mom wasn't having it. She was adamant about me going to the revival in Memphis, TN at our pastor's other church. It was a tug of war that night of me saying to her "No, I have plans" and her saying, "Oh, you are going to church." I was determined with a no, but she ended up winning. I got dressed that night in a red dress. The evangelist spoke a word and then called people to come to the altar for prayer. I was the one that never turned down a good prayer. I wasn't saved, but I wasn't stupid either. I needed Jesus. I got in the line. It was a long line but finally it was my time for prayer. You know what this man did? He stopped the line and said, "Who wants to be saved." I kid you not. That left hand of mine went up without telling me. It was as if someone else threw it up for me. Prior to that night, the Lord had been dealing with me in my dorm room. He was calling me back to Him and that night in late September was the night for me to completely surrender. The evangelist said, "No wonder the Lord had me stop this line." That man laid hands on me and it was over. The power of God hit me. That is where I got my "Yes" and I've had it ever since. I surrendered completely to the Lord. However, that is not the end of my story. When I came to myself and really gave thought to what had happened. I was still at the front of the church. I began to wrestle in my mind. "What am I going to do about my boyfriend?" It was a real battle. Then, the Lord sent an evangelist missionary to whisper these words in my ear. "Sister, the Lord said that He is going to send you a husband."

Wait! What? How did she know I was battling with that in my mind? She knew nothing about me. Therefore, it had to be the Lord revealing it to her. Those words resonated within me, and my feet got the news. I began to run and dance and praise God. I believed the report through her from the Lord. That night, I praised God for my husband. God had in reserve for me a good man that had the same drive that I did. He sent a good man to walk this journey with me. God made us one. What happened to me happened to him. He was there the entire time hurting like I was. So, this next chapter is written by my husband, Erskine. Let's learn of how he endured this journey his way, in silence.

CHAPTER TWO
SUFFERING IN SILENCE

by Erskine Murphy

As I reflect on the circumstances and current state of affairs that are happening in the world, this country, this state, this city, and this town, I ponder on the conditions of what seems to have become a normal day to see death after death. A state where just as many young people are dying as are elderly people. These are people who are supposedly just getting ready to spread their wings and see what life has to offer them. These are young people who will never experience getting married, having children, having grandkids, or living a long life with the ones they love. This condition that I see the world in makes me wonder how Mariah Yvette Murphy would have been. Who would she look like? Who would she act more like? What type of personality would she have? How would she have impacted our lives?

As a father expecting the birth of his first child, I was left speechless. There has never been a more vivid look of pain, of discouragement, of complete loss for words and what can be accounted as a loss of hope. The pain that says more than a million words. The pain that no words of comfort, no words from a preacher, a therapist, a psychologist, or a loving parent could render would ease it or make it go away. So, what do you do when you feel so much pain? What do you do when you see so much pain? As a husband, seeing the pain of my wife, all I asked was, what do I do? What do I say?

Some may say that is important for grief to be shared, grief to be distributed so that the burdens are not solely carried by one person. There may be some accuracy to that saying; however, there are instances where one must understand that some grief has to be borne alone. I didn't want to make things harder for my wife, but time and a relationship with the Lord helped me to stand. One of my favorite scriptures is Jeremiah 17:7 KJV which states, "Blessed is the man that trusteth in the Lord, and whose hope the Lord is." I had to learn to put my trust and confidence in the Lord. I learned to lean on Him through the good times and the bad.

Through the years, the saying that time heals all wounds has become more apparent. The scars from the wounds are still there. The picture of the day is still there and can be replayed at any moment. Some things can be erased and forgotten. However, this moment of pain has been imprinted within me. It is a part of who I am now. Who I have become. There is no erasing it. However, I can say that the pain isn't the same, but the thoughts of what if, the thoughts of what could have been, the thoughts of where would she be now, what would she be doing and would she have kids, those thoughts, have over time replaced the pain of that day for me as her father.

The hurt, the pain, the tears, the look of why, the look of how, the look of "I have been faithful to You, God," and the look of "I cannot believe this is happening to me" is so surreal. It left me with a question from that day as I suffered in silence, of where do we go from here?

LET'S PRAY

Lord, I pray for fathers as they face the challenges of this day. Our men are so important in their roles as father figures to give guidance to not only their children but other children that do not have that role model. Father, I pray for strength and knowledge over each of them as they instruct and protect those that are around them. I pray that You cover them and help them to stand up to be the men that You are calling them to be. I pray strategies and clarity of thought over them. I pray for wisdom and discernment. I pray for peace and a prayer life. Lord, build them up in You. Steer them in the direction that You would have them to go even as they ask that all too familiar question, "Where do we go from here?" Encourage them to know that their answers to the "Where" are always in You as they seek You. You will lead them, for Your Word declares it. Thank You for being the Way, the Truth and the Life.

Oh, it is in Jesus' Name that I pray. Amen.

TO WHOM WOULD WE GO?

"Then Jesus turned to the Twelve and asked, 'Are you also going to leave?'

Simon Peter replied, 'Lord, to whom would we go? You have the words that give eternal life.

We believe, and we know you are the Holy One of God.'"

John 6:67-69 NLT

At this point in both Hannah's lives, the question really became, what now? Was their relationship solid enough with the Lord to stand the testing or were they going to leave Jesus?

In the scripture above, Peter had walked with Jesus long enough to understand the truths that Jesus was explaining to the people in the previous verses of this chapter. What Jesus said was hard for them to grasp and He knew it, but they needed to know more than just miracles, signs, and wonders. They needed to know His love for them. They needed to understand His purpose for coming. They needed to develop strength and endurance as hard times came. When He went deeper into who He was and what He could provide to them, they could not make sense of it. So, they left. That is why it is so important to develop a relationship with Jesus. I've heard people say this many times before: "God, I seek Your Face and not Your Hand." Do you really?

This is a life-long journey that requires communion with our Savior. We must get to know Him and not just want what He can do for us or give to us.

Jesus had proven who He was to them, and there is still no one else to call upon. He is the same today, yesterday, and forever more. There was no one else to turn to. Jesus was the Christ. He was their way to Father God. So, when Jesus asked the Twelve, "Are you also going to leave," knowing what they knew from experience, there was only one answer to give. There was no one better or greater than Jesus. He was everything they needed.

For the Hannahs, we were face to face with our realities. Like Peter and the apostles, we had to make conscious decisions of how we would handle our situations. The choice was ours. What the Lord had allowed had to be accepted, period. So, I imagine Jesus asking the Hannahs, "Are you also going to leave?" Although we could have answered that question with a yes and given various reasons why, we knew He was the way. He was our answer. So, we chose Him and answered His question with a question by asking, "Where do we go from here?"

CHAPTER THREE
WHERE DO WE GO FROM HERE?

He needs you to survive.

Life had brought some upsetting blows to us [the Hannahs] and God had allowed them to happen. How could a God so loving, so rich in mercy, so full of joy, so able to do anything but fail, allow such horrific things to happen to His daughters? How?!

We have all asked that question. Even now, we, as His children, are still experiencing devasting blows. Death (the loss of a precious loved one), betrayal (being deceived by someone you thought would always have your back), unemployment (unable to pay your bills and take care of your family), sickness (doctor gives you some devastating news), just all types of storms that if you don't watch it, you can easily find yourself outside the Will of God, giving up, getting off track, or even cracking under the pressure.

We are hit with all types of issues that seem to have a domino effect where one thing happens after the next or a hurricane effect where everything is twisted and turned and tossed everywhere seemingly all at once. The book of Job described this as "Trouble." Job 14:1 KJV says, "Man that is born of a woman is of few days and full of trouble."

Trouble is described as difficulty, unrest, disorder, anxiety, or distress. It's an uninvited guest that tries to stick around and make itself at home. It tries to put its feet up on your coffee table or get comfortable in your bed under your covers. It even tries to go to your refrigerator and eat up your food, just making itself at home with you. None of us are exempt from Old Man Trouble – he's good at his job. If trouble had a voice and had a chance to describe itself, it would tell you arrogantly, "Man, I was created for this. I am an expert in my field. I'm one of a kind and I don't mind showing up."

Yeah, trouble can wreak havoc, causing widespread destruction in your life. We can't opt out of trouble. We are not exempt from it. We can't run from it. It will find you in that due season, in due time.

As a child, I remember Pastor Lonnie M. Haley telling us a story about trouble in a message one Sunday. He said that there was this man trying to outrun trouble. So, he got on a bus and traveled to a place where he thought trouble couldn't find him. When he made it to his destination, trouble was right there at that bus stop. When he got off the bus, trouble told him that he had been waiting on him and that he had gotten off just where he expected him to.

When trouble comes, it may seem as if you can't make it through, but know that the Lord allowed it for your good. You may not be able to understand it at the time, but be encouraged to press through, all the while seeing your salvation, seeing your deliverance, seeing that light at the end of the tunnel. God wants to put something in you that will push and even propel you to your next level in Him.

> *God is craving a deeper relationship with us. Don't just scratch the surface. There is so much to God. He will take you high above your circumstances where you can rest in Him. Remember, as the Word of God instructs in Acts 17:28a KJV, "For in Him we live and move, and have our being..." Giving Him your life (repenting of your sins) is just the beginning. Learn of God and allow Him to teach you to walk in His fullness. That fullness means learning everything about Him, the complete package, every aspect of who He is. That includes His Word, His Ways, His Glory, and His Power. Knowing who He is will allow you to easily retreat to Him and take refuge not only in the time of trouble but all the time just because you want to be in His Presence. This is when you will really experience the fullness of God.*

One thing about the enemy, he wants us to focus in on our troubles. He wants us to nurture them and dwell on them, or just give up and die, but don't let that be the end of your story. Job's wife suggested that he (Job) turn his back on his God and give up on life. Had Job heeded her suggestions, he never would have seen what God had for him after his great trial. He never would have had his Job chapter 42 experience. After that great test was over, the Lord could still testify of Job and say as He did in Job 1:8 KJV, "…hast thou considered my servant Job, that there is none like him in the earth, a perfect and an upright man, one that feareth God, and escheweth evil?"

Can God testify for you? Do you have the endurance to go through like Job and yet trust in God?

God needs you to survive this thing you are facing. Know that you are not alone. Let Him direct your path. You are His hands. You are His feet. He needs you! Stop asking why and find out why by seeking Him. Pray and seek His Face. Get to that point where you say, "God, I want to survive. Lord, help me to survive. Here I am Lord, show me the way. Get me to that place in You where I can move forward. Help me!"

Cry out to Him! Allow him to minister to your hurt. He specializes in the Ministry of Hurt. He has a way of getting to the root and pulling out everything that has you bound. He has a way of healing your heart. Trust His plan for your life. Give Him full control. Build up your faith in Him. Be determined that truly "No weapon formed against you shall prosper..." (Isaiah 54:17 KJV).

Regardless of the Bs in your life, God sees you as a Beatitude.

Whether you are broken, beaten, bruised, betrayed, bewildered, battered, blackened, blocked, blistered, buttoned, bottomed out, blinded, blemished, blotted, blighted, bent, bleeding, bashed, bland, banned, or blue, God calls you BLESSED!!!! You are a Beatitude!!

> *Jeremiah 1:10 KJV declares, "See, I have this day set thee over the nations and over the kingdoms, to root out, and to pull down, and to destroy, and to throw down, to build, and to plant."*

Oh, my friends, there is much to be done. Allow your gifts to make room for you. God is only trying to build you into a strong vessel for Him to do Jeremiah 1:10. I've heard over the years, that it doesn't take all of that. Well, my questions for those that are saying that are, "Where are you trying to go? What are you trying to do?" You can't please yourself and God too. Self has to die. God is trying to get us to a place where we can walk out Jeremiah 1:10. We go through the valley. We are not to quit or stop midstream. We go through because God is with us even when it seems He is not. He is Omnipresent. He is there. He is our Jehovah Shammah, meaning the Lord Is There. He may be quiet at times and even feel distant, but He is there!

Some years ago, I remember being in a situation. As a missionary, a prayer warrior, people are always asking for prayer. "Pray for me!" "Pray for me!" "Remember me in your prayers." Don't get me wrong. That is perfectly fine. That is what I am called to do. I take pleasure in knowing that people believe in my prayer ministry. However, being in the midst of this particular situation, I saw myself in the spirit realm adorned in a robe with a long train. On the train of the robe, there were many people and all their cares, their requests plus mine. It was so heavy. It pulled on my shoulders. What I saw in the spirit realm was starting to affect me in the natural realm. It drained me physically. I saw that I could barely walk, and I was just dragging, trying to keep the robe on and keep the prayer ministry going. It got heavier and heavier. It appeared that I was carrying way more than I needed to. However, the real problem was that I wasn't emptying out. I was holding everything myself. I wasn't giving it to the Lord even when I thought I was. This was one of those moments that I should have said as the disciples said to Jesus, "Lord, teach me to pray" (Luke 11:1 KJV). Lord, teach me how to pray where I will give it all to You and not try to fix it myself. Lord, teach me how to pray so they can see You and not me. Lord, teach me how to pray where Your Will can be done and not mine.

Finally, I couldn't take anymore. Something had to give. I remember praying right before leaving for work one morning, "LORD, HELP ME!!!" I was bent over, saying, "It's so heavy God. Help me!!" It was there that I did what I should have done all along. I gave it all to God. I had to cast it all upon the Lord. I had to let it go and allow God to move. He was teaching me in that moment. I wanted to fix it. Everywhere I looked, I saw brokenness, calamity, chaos, unrest, but it wasn't mines to fix. It was for me to carry to the Lord. I thought I was doing that, but I was still holding on, trying to make things better. I was trying to keep things together. That was not God's plan for me. His plan was to show me that He was my Jehovah Shammah, and it started with me fully trusting Him. From this experience, I found that He was doing some rooting out and plucking up of His own within me. I had to get to the mindset of "not my will, Lord, but Thy will be done." Matthew 10:39 NLT states, "If you cling to your life, you will lose it; but if you give up your life for me, you will find it." This is not only how I survived this situation; this is how the Hannahs survived too. We gave up ourselves and found a new life through worship and trust in God.

Oh, my friends, He needs you to survive. Ask God for direction right where you are. Ask Him to direct your path. Get out of your own way. Tampering with it and trying to fix it yourself only slows down the process. You must give

Him full control. You must trust Him to handle it. You are hindering your own progression by continuing to worry and focus on the trouble. It is important to remember that God can take control and alter your situation much faster and far better than you can even imagine. But you must give it to Him. We cannot allow the fear of not knowing what God is going to do, how fast He is going to do it, or what direction He is going to take it in, to stop or postpone our progress or success. We just have to trust and know that, in the end, the decision that He makes is in our best interest. He knows best. So, give God the right of way in your life. That is when you will begin to see the light at the end of the tunnel. No matter where you are on your life's journey, keep Him first. How many times have you had to make a choice and you knew the right way, but chose the other way because it looked better? Oh, I speak to you today, to choose the way of God. It is almost guaranteed not to be the most popular way. Others will have gone another way, but save yourself some heartache and obey God. Yes, you may get talked about, but ask yourself what is really in the hearts of the talkers. Do they have a form of godliness? Are they trying to justify their choices by getting others to join their way? Choose God. Let people think what they will. Proverbs 14:12 KJV says, "There is a way that seems right to a man, but its end is the way of death." Oh, my friend, choose God's way. His path gets you to that destination that He promised.

You will survive whatever you are facing. It may seem lonely on this way, but that is all right. In John 16:32 KJV, Jesus said, "Behold, the hour cometh, yea, is now come, that ye shall be scattered, every man to his own, and shall leave me alone: and yet I am not alone, because the Father is with me." What a powerful scripture! Jesus is the perfect example here. He knew Father God was with Him during His hardest moments. You are to know the same. Draw closer to God. The closer you draw to Him, the less alone you will feel. You will hear Him speaking to you about yourself and even about others. You will find yourself giving others a Word from the Lord that will encourage them. So, know this; not only does the Lord need you to survive, the people need you to survive. Oh, I feel victory. Expect it!!!

At the time of Hannah One's trial, she didn't know God's plan for her life. She didn't know that one day she would have the privilege of carrying a prophet named Samuel who would be called and used of God greatly. In the eyes of the people, Samuel would be a man of honor, integrity and obedience. God would use him to anoint Saul and David as kings. God would use him as a religious judge for the people. He would be a great man of God. Like his mother, he would be a great prayer warrior. His prayer life would reveal to us how God heard him and moved mightily.

In the book of 1 Samuel 7:1-13 KJV, we see a great example of who Samuel would be. These scriptures tell of a time when the children of Israel felt abandoned by God, and rightly so; they had turned to serving other gods. What did they expect, a God that would say, "Do whatever you want to do? I don't mind." No, God forbid. He is a just and forgiving God, but He requires our commitment. They should have felt abandoned. That feeling of abandonment was the path they needed to take to lead them to repentance. God had Samuel on that path, and He used Samuel to call the people back to Him. Samuel told them to put away their strange gods and return unto the Lord, serving Him only. Then, he called them together to fast and pray before the Lord. When their enemy, the Philistines, heard they were all together, they devised a plan of attack to take God's people out. We already know that when we fast, over time, we become physically weak but spiritually stronger. The Philistine army came to attack Samuel and the Israelites when they were in a vulnerable state physically, but their timing couldn't have been more perfect. 2 Chronicles 7:14 KJV describes exactly what was going on. It declares, "If my people, which are called by my name, shall humble themselves, and pray, and seek my face, and turn from their wicked ways; then will I hear from heaven, and will forgive their sin, and will heal their land." That day, Samuel, Hannah One's son, cried out to the Lord and the Lord delivered them from their enemy. The Bible goes on to declare in those same scriptures that the hand of the Lord was against the Philistines all the days of Samuel.

Oh, my friends, God's protection for Samuel was guaranteed. Why? Because 2 Chronicles 7:14 was a promise from God. Samuel did his part. He served the Lord wholeheartedly. We can't expect God to deliver us with our hearts far from Him. However, that is what the Israelites were doing. They worshiped other gods. Before Eli the priest died, the Israelites were fighting the Philistines, but they were unable to defeat them because God was not with them. It took Samuel to speak up and tell them to get rid of their idol gods and serve the Lord only. That is when their deliverance came.

> *So now, we can see why Hannah needed to persevere. She couldn't see it at the time, but better days were coming. She just had to hold out and use the source she had. For although her husband wanted to be that source of comfort and relieve her grief, that wasn't his place. God was showing her Himself as her only source and comfort.*

I know it is our nature to pray that we don't have to go through the battles of life, but the fact of the matter is that we will go through them. However, how we go through plays a very important role. Look at it this way; we should rather be in right fellowship with the Lord and have Him fighting for us being our Jehovah Shammah than to be in the fight alone.

God would raise up a mighty prophet through Hannah One, whom He would use greatly to save His people. Actually, God raised up Hannah One first, a great woman of

God that displayed trust and hope in her God. What she was going through was all a part of God's plan. It brought her to some of her lowest moments, but when you have a desire planted by God on the inside, the "where do we go from here" question gets answered with one word - Up. Hannah had the odds stacked against her from her viewpoint, but still, she had to allow that strong desire that weighed so heavy to be enough to produce the results she wanted. She didn't know God had purposely shut up her womb. She just knew she wanted a baby. She didn't know that every triumph against her enemies was drawing her closer to her womb being opened. She just wanted to share in the joy of motherhood. So, she took what she knew about her God and prayed a prayer that would change things forever. She went further than most mothers would. She prayed a sacrificial promise, a gift to be given to her to present back to her God. Even though she was blind to her future, her longing to be complete pushed her to keep going, because something greater was coming out of her pain.

So, I ask, what has God called you to do? What is God's plan for you? Like many of the men and women in the Bible, obeying and living out His plan will not only be a blessing to you but to others after you, generations and generations to come. Think about it; these Bible stories are still encouraging us today. The perseverance of men and women of the Bible has inspired so many to see their trials to the end. What a blessing to have the Word of God, the Bible, as our guide. I am. You are. We are left without an excuse.

After rededicating my life to the Lord (Hannah Two) at the age of 19, I surrounded myself with the older mothers. They prayed all the time. At the time, I just loved their commitment to God. I did not ask them the why, the what, the who, the when, or the how they were so committed to prayer. I was just drawn to it and consumed myself in it. However, over the years, I learned. They were enduring hard trials like good soldiers. Prayer was their way to victory. Unity at the altar was their way to answered prayers. Commitment was their way to survival.

As I reminisce on those prayers, one person would pray after another. This would go on and on. After a long while, the prayer would get quiet. Then, the Church Mother would say, "Pray through, saints, pray through." To me then, those words only meant keep praying until we are done with this prayer hour. However, "pray through" to me now has taken on a whole new meaning. Praying through requires endurance and faith. It's a whole lot more than getting to the end of an hour of prayer time. It means enduring in faith for the breakthrough. It means seeing the trial through to the end, trusting God.

Those women shared their testimonies of triumph. When I look back at what they endured, I see their strength, their courage, and their hope in God. I understand now why they would cry out spontaneously in the service "Hope!" That hope said, despite all of what I am going through, I have a God that will see me through. I have a God that will uphold me with the right hand of His righteousness! I have a God that cannot fail.

So, I ask, after we have prayed and endured and survived, where do we go from here? Beloved, there is no question about it. We go where our hope is and cleave to Him with all our might. Hope thou in God!

LET'S PRAY

Dear Heavenly Father,

I pray for this your son, your daughter. You see their need right now. Father, I ask that You touch them and give them the strength they need to remain steadfast and committed to You. I know that You have a plan for their lives. Help them to see it all the way through. Help them to endure to see their victories all the way to the end. Dear Lord, Moses only got to look towards and see the Promise. However, Lord, I ask that You help them to experience their promises and walk in them.

Oh, I declare victory over my sister. I declare peace over my brother. I speak life to this reader now. I call encouragement to come upon them now. I declare that they will make it. They will survive.

So, thank You Father, for answering this prayer. Thank You for helping them to cast their cares upon You. Thank You for the hope and joy and peace that they feel overtaking them even as they read these words of prayer. I thank You now. It is in Jesus' Name that I pray. Thank God, Amen.

Why art thou cast down, O my soul?

And why art thou disquieted in me?

Hope thou in God: for I shall yet praise him for the help of his countenance.

Psalms 42:5 KJV

Some things can shake our very core and cause us to be in an uproar. The Psalmist here is asking himself, why are you in such a rage? Why are you so troubled? Why so much noise? Seek the quietness of God. Hope in God, and with His help, drown out the noise.

CHAPTER FOUR
DROWN OUT THE NOISE

When we go through, it seems many will have an opinion of what should have been done. Some will even tell you what they think you did wrong that caused the situation. No encouragement, just noise. However, that is not the worst of it. That is not the only noise. There is also a war of the mind. Yes, I called it the enemy of the mind in the introduction. A constant flood of negative thoughts, the "should've, could've, if only I would've" noises that can be even more devastating than what someone else could say. Over and over in your mind, wondering when things changed that took you down this path leading you head-on to this devastation. *Did I miss a warning sign? When did I overdo it? Did someone wish this bad thing upon me? Did I sin? What did I do to deserve this terrible tragedy in my life? What did I do wrong? Am I that bad?*

Things are not quiet. They are far from quiet, but yet we still walk around with a façade out of this world trying to hide what's really going on inside.. We are geniuses at disguising our true feelings, finding the right mask for the day to match our outfits. But the Psalmist in Psalm 42 is saying, "Hope thou in God." Take off the masks. Stop putting on the fronts and show God the true you. Don't cover it up. Don't sweep it under the rug. Don't hold it in. Let God show you how to grow from even this horrendous thing. Allow God to minister to your hurt. He already knows. He knows the way you take. He is waiting for you to cry out for help like Peter did when Jesus allowed him to come join Him walking on the water. Even in those moments of knowing that Jesus is right there, yet our faith grows weak, and we begin to sink. I assure you that He is right there to immediately rescue you. Trust me, He loves you so much. He will not let you drown even when it feels like you are already under water and are just one breath from death. Hope yet in God. Thinking back on 1 Samuel Chapter 7 mentioned in the previous chapter, the children of Israel were telling Prophet Samuel to cry out for them. They knew Samuel was a righteous man. His walk with God proved it. They knew his ways pleased the Lord. Their hope was once again in the Lord to see them through. They had too many testimonies of victory. They needed God to answer in that very moment. They needed a right-now deliverance. Thank God, the Lord came to their rescue.

Oh, I advise you today. Do not worry about who is watching. There is a cry from the Spirit Realm for you saying, "Come to Me. Come, let Me heal you. Come, let Me show you great and mighty things that you know not of. Enter into My rest." You must drown out those that have held you back for far too long. You must get your promise in view and fix your focus on it. Do not allow outside influences to become inside distractions. That is, do not allow those outside of God's purpose and will for you to affect you and cause mental distractions. Allow God's influences to propel your mentality to press on to your promise.

God knows how to get you in the right position for healing. He has connections. He will send the right people to minister to you who will say the right things to help drown out the noises of the enemy of your mind. They are servants of the Most High called to speak life to you and make declarations over you that will pull you up and out of the pits and prisons that have you bound, thus releasing you from the chains and fetters that have paralyzed your faith. They are equipped with longevity and endurance. They are there for the long haul, sisters and brothers whom God has gifted and anointed to speak over your life until you are in a place where you can once again speak life over yourself. As I looked back over my life, God has used various people to speak into my life. As you are reading this book, you will find some of the prophesies. God used His servants as couriers. The words that they spoke over me were dispatched strategically for specific times in my life when I needed help to get to that next level in God. Their words were like nuggets that encouraged me to keep my focus on the prize.

Oh, just as the Lord called me, God is calling you as

well to come up, and it starts with a willingness to do it. He allowed all of it for a reason. Know that someone needs to hear your testimony. They need to hear not only what happened, but how you made it through, so that they can overcome their situations too. Revelation 12:11 KJV, "And they overcame him by the blood of the Lamb, and by the word of their testimony." We have the promise of God that we will be victorious because of the Blood of Jesus, and it is our witness to others that will not only give us overwhelming victory, but that victory will be for all who hears it and believes. So, allow God to put you in that spiritual place where you can grow from what you and others have been through.

Will the noises stop? Yes, they can stop. It's up to you. 1 Peter 5:8 KJV declares, "Be sober, be vigilant; because your adversary the devil, as a roaring lion, walketh about seeking whom he may devour." He is always at his job. He will not stop, because he wants to block your testimony. Remember, he comes to steal, kill, and destroy, period. When he can't get you one way, know that he is looking to come from other angles. He never stops trying to destroy your potential. His intentions are to block where God wants to take you. Sometimes the attacks will come simultaneously. Your job, your children, your spouse, your church, your family, none of these areas are exempt from attacks. Everything and everyone attached to you is under his radar. Oh, but you have authority and power over the enemy. So, use it. That is why it is crucial for us to stay on guard spiritually. This counterattacks the noises. We need to have spiritual senses that are keen, strong, and powerful. Ephesians 5:15 NIV says, "Be very careful, then, how you live—not as unwise but as wise." Staying spiritually sober, watchful, and alert is wisdom. Your enemy could strike at any moment. So, we must be sensitive to the Spirit of God. What is the Holy Spirit saying? What are you dreaming? What visions are you having? What is the Lord showing you in the Spirit? When we focus on and do what God is saying, we won't fall prey to the devil's tactics. 1 Peter 5:9 KJV admonishes us to resist the devil and be steadfast in being resistant. That means be constant, committed, and determined in your faith. Use your weapons (the Word of God and prayer) and stay strong.

One day, I was on my way to work. I sensed that an attack was set in motion for me that day in the form of some type of accident. I didn't call anyone. I just asked the Lord to dispatch His warring angels around my vehicle and I began to pray in the spirit. I was on guard the entire ride, praying and staying alert. I remained in prayer until the feeling of an attack left. The Lord never revealed what was going on, but I sensed in the spirit that angels were fighting for me. My spiritual sense of feeling was on, and I thank God that I stayed focused. We won.

There have been times that I heard the Lord say what type of demonic spirit was trying to invade my space. I must admit, the first time I experienced this, I ignored it. I heard the word, "Suicide" just as plain as anything. My spiritual sense of hearing was on point, but what I heard did not make sense to me. I was thinking, surely that is not the case in my house, but I was wrong. It soon manifested just as the Holy Spirit had revealed and I missed it. I was disappointed in myself because I did not heed the warning that He so clearly gave. There was no question, no room for doubt, but I did both. I questioned and doubted. The Lord said it. Warning came before destruction. I just ignored it because it didn't make sense. I did not want to accept the fact that this foreign thing was coming to attack and invade my world. I did not go into war mode. I didn't ask the Lord to give me clarity on what I heard. I didn't pray about it. I didn't ask who it was in my house being attacked. I went into denial. What I saw with my natural eyes did not agree with what I heard in the Spirit. It was as if I was saying to the demonic spirit, "Come on in. Have a seat. Want something to drink?" To me, not heeding the warning was like inviting it in.

When it manifested, I immediately thought of what the Spirit of the Lord had said. I remembered where I was when He said it. Oh, but thank God for stored-up prayers and for saving my position on the front line, because believe you me, I was late, but I showed up armed and ready. Once again, we won, and we will always win. 2 Corinthians 2:14a GW states, "But I thank God, who always leads us in victory because of Christ." So, like the elderly mothers used to say to me when I was growing up, allow me to admonish the same to you and say, "Stay with the Lord!

Stay with Him!"

My friend, He is more than the whole world against you even when it seems like He is nowhere to be found. He is there. In those times of feeling all alone, the noises will probably be very loud. Just remember, you don't have to hear them. God is ready to take us higher in Him. It is in that higher place where He will reveal to us that the noise is no longer affecting us.

LET'S PRAY

Dear Lord,

You specialize in taking us higher. It gets so noisy down here, especially in times of trouble. It gets hard to even hear You because of all the chaos surrounding us. But Lord, I am thankful for Your Word that declares in Psalms 61:2 KJV: "From the end of the earth will I cry unto thee, when my heart is overwhelmed: lead me to the rock that is higher than I."

Lord, as my Rock, You know how to lead me in that plain path.[1] Lord, You know how to be that lamp unto my feet and that light unto my pathway.[2] Lead me, Lord. Take me higher in You. Drown out the noise and help me to view this situation from a higher level. I know if I go higher, what I see will change. What I hear will change. Even what I feel will change. It won't seem so big, and my focus, my perception will change from it to You.

Oh Father, I look for deliverance today. Have Your way in me. Have Your Own way! You have the right of way. You are first. For I know that my yielding to You and my endurance will bring forth a better me in the end. It is in Jesus' Name that I pray. Amen.

PROPHECY RECEIVED IN JULY 2021

The Lord said, "Go deeper to go higher."

Wow! Those words were like fire in my bones. They lit a torch in me. I went to minister at a church and the title of my message was "Hannah, Get Up!" This was the first time I went into depth of what happened with my first pregnancy. It was hard to tell it. I cried through the entire testimony. Little did I know that God was birthing a new Marilyn that day. A lady named Lakeeda Thomas came up to me after service and said that the Lord said, "Go deeper to go higher." Those words changed my life. I held them close. They were precious to me. They hit at the core of my being. I knew it was a Word from the Lord. I pondered on them for months. I shared it with others, and I did what it said do. I was already on my face seeking God, but I went deeper. I went into the position of seek.

CHAPTER FIVE

INTO THE POSITION OF SEEK

Both Hannahs were at a point of desperation. They needed God. For Hannah One, she did what she knew to do. She made her way to the House of God. The taunting, the torment, the bullying all propelled her to the only help she knew. Her worship was for real. There, she began to pour out to God saying, "Lord, look on my affliction. Remember me. Give me the desires of my heart. Lord, if You give me a man child, I'll give him back to You." Bless me indeed oh God!! Enlarge my tents.

Hannah prayed out of her heart. I mean, she went in. She got out all she needed to. She was releasing and casting all her cares upon the One Who cared for her. She was crying out to God in a real way, in her own way. This was where she needed to be. This was the position God was trying to get her in. She was called to wail. This wail would confront all the torture, the grief, the anger, and the sadness that was built up in her. It didn't matter who was watching. She had drowned out the noise. She ignored the distractions and cried out for help. She prayed until only her lips moved. She had moved from an audible cry to a spiritual cry from the depths of her being.

She was in the position of seek. Pleasing others was no longer on her agenda. Remaining quiet and reserved was no longer at the forefront, dominating her demeanor. She moved out of desperation. Her need was her focal point. Her surroundings didn't matter. Her need for an answer took her out of herself. She went after God. She wanted God to do it. This worship from her grabbed the attention of the priest (Eli). He observed her and thought she was drunk. He judged her from a physical standpoint. He judged her out of tradition. He was used to hearing a voice during prayer and approached her from that place of tradition. But thank God, she was in the Spirit and God saw her where she was. She responded to Eli the priest, "No, my lord, I am a woman of a sorrowful spirit: I have drunk neither wine nor strong drink, but have poured out my soul before the LORD. Count not thine handmaid for a daughter of Belial: for out of the abundance of my complaint and grief have I spoken hitherto." (1 Samuel 1:15 KJV)

Eli perceived incorrectly. He was on the outside looking in. It is obvious that he was blinded by his traditions and they prevented him from seeing clearly. Traditions can have us so out of focus and unable to see that its really God that is working. Perhaps this was his first time seeing someone pray from the depths of their being. In the natural, he could not see that she came to pour out her praise on the altar. She was there to pour her worship upon the One who had the answer. She came expecting an answer. Her need drew her to her God, and He heard her. So profoundly does Psalm 61:1-3 KJV express Hannah One's position at that time as it declares, "Hear my cry, O God; attend unto my prayer. From the end of the earth will I cry unto thee, when my heart is overwhelmed: lead me to the rock that is higher than I. For thou hast been a shelter for me, and a strong tower from the enemy."

God was drawn to her cry. Her position pulled Him into her need. Her worship brought forth His Presence. Her sound grasped His attention and He responded. God moved upon Hannah One that day. Although her voice had no sound, He heard her loud and clear in the Spirit.

> *Psalm 86:6 KJV says, "Give ear, O Lord, unto my prayer; and attend to the voice of my supplications." Wait, do my supplications have a voice? Do my prayers have a sound? Oh, yes! There is a voice with a sound, a distinct sound you have that you need to get to. Find it and use it. Worship the Lord in the beauty of holiness[1]. Go deep in your worship. It gets His attention. Make His praise glorious![2] Glorify Him! Tell Him that you adore Him. Tell Him that you love Him! Tell Him that you are lost without Him. This is how you worship Him!*

That is what Hannah One did and, in those moments, once she revealed her purpose to him, Priest Eli understood. He saw that she was not playing. God opened his eyes where he could see her pure heart. Then God used him to assure her that her God had heard her. Eli told her to go in peace, that the God of Israel would grant her the petition that she asked of Him. The priest's words brought the confirmation she needed. It was as if she literally grabbed his words and ran with them. She had broken through and received her answer. She had prayed through. This was like a touching the hem of Jesus' garment moment. The virtue of God came out of that hem and turned her situation because of her faith. The anointing of God destroyed that thing that was destroying her. The Lord had turned her captivity. Her prayers were answered. It was at this moment that Hannah One was elevated to another level. Her faith had made her whole. She believed the report of the Lord. She found the faith she needed, and she activated it. Her position of seek had taken her higher. Her journey home with the family would be different. Her walk was different. Her interaction with Peninnah and the kids was different. Elkanah got his wife back. She was laughing and full of joy because she prayed until she got her breakthrough. The days of Peninnah's intimidation getting the best of her were behind her.

This reminds me of an old praise song that we used to sing at church after someone would share a testimony of the goodness of the Lord. "I got just what I wanted. I got just what I wanted. I got just what I wanted from the Lord. I got just what I wanted. I got just what I wanted from the Lord." They would go on to sing, "Deliverance is what I wanted. Deliverance is what I wanted. Deliverance is what I wanted from the Lord. Deliverance is what I wanted. Deliverance is what I wanted. Deliverance is what I wanted from the Lord."

Oh, my friends, this is a journey. We can't go into the position of seek and not expect God to move upon us, deliver us, and take us higher. He repositions us for new levels. He repositions us for our NEXT!

Hannah One was on her way to her deliverance. She wasn't at the finish line yet. She understood it was a process, but within herself, she knew she was barren no more. Ah, but mind you this, when we increase in faith and receive a yes from God, it doesn't mean that our enemies will stop their evil ways. A snake is still a snake. The hissing may get worse. The taunts may increase. More distractions may come. The enemy may launch everything he has at us, but the fact of the matter is we've moved. What worked before no longer has that same effect on us because God has moved us. Any final grip that Satan has must release us, because he cannot go where God is taking us. God takes us higher.

Although I weep telling my story 25+ years later, I am elated to say, my stillborn baby was not the end of my story. I, Hannah Two, had to go into the position of seek just like Hannah One. It took a long time for me to let Mariah go mentally so I could move on with my life with my husband. I thought of her every day, all while trying to get pregnant again. But nothing. I wanted to keep her memory alive. So, I used her name as part of my passwords. I used any way I could to keep her memory alive. I wasn't ready to let her go. I yearned for her and desired another baby with a torn heart. I battled thoughts like, "God, I am still saved. I am doing what is right. Why can't I get pregnant? Other women were getting pregnant right after having a baby and some are not even married. What am I doing wrong? Have You forsaken me?" I waited and waited and waited, but nothing. Months passed by but still nothing. However, like Job, I did not charge God foolishly. I kept believing that it would happen. After all, I had the promise. I had the prophecy.

Seriously though, was there something wrong with me? No. My problem was I still needed to heal emotionally. I was grieving. I had felt the kicks, the movements and I received so much joy from them and they abruptly stopped. My expectations even of the birthing process all changed from this devastating news. I was this young woman that really hadn't experienced real hurt until this occurred, and it seemed like no one understood why I couldn't snap out of it.

Although, life kept moving, it was like I was stuck in that moment of hearing, "I'm sorry, Mrs. Murphy." I still had a very vivid memory of my baby's lifeless body floating in me. I was smiling on the outside and crushed on the inside. I became a subject matter expert on how to cry on the inside. Thankfully, there was one thing that did not stop. I was always hearing from the Lord. The Holy Spirit was there all the time, comforting me. He was speaking to me personally. He was even speaking to me through others. At the time, LaShun Pace had put out an [1]album titled, "Wealthy Place."[3] I played it over and over, because the Lord was speaking clearly to me saying, "I am going to put you in a wealthy place." I heard it so plainly. Doors began to open for me. I graduated with an associate's degree and got a new job. When I walked into the building at my new place of employment, there was marble on the walls. The Holy Spirit quickly reminded me of what He said. It was the beginning of my healing, of my wealthy place, but still the question remained. God, what about my children? The promise was there, but no babies. Time continued. It felt like I had a hole in my heart, and I knew that only God could fill it. He was working on it. What He was trying to get me to understand was that He needed me in the right place mentally to receive my healing so that I could move on and experience all that He had for me.

Now that I look back, I was not ready for children. I see it clearly. I really needed a healing from God. I had to let everything that I had gone through go. I had to let Mariah go. I couldn't see how bad it was. However, I suppose everyone else did.

Finally, one Sunday, we were at a regular church service. The speaker was Elder Grady Henderson, Jr. He ministered the Word of the Lord and then asked if anyone wanted prayer. My husband, the suffering in silence one, came and got me and took me up for prayer. It seemed that the saints got happy. Oh, my God! I thank God for my husband. Elder Henderson began to pray for me and said, "Marilyn, you have to let her go. Let it go, Marilyn." His hand was on my head, and he was praying hard. He was my Priest Eli. He spoke life over me and prayed blessings over me. He prophesied over me and told me that everything would be all right.

That is the last time I remember someone praying for me about it. Honestly, I don't know when I let go. I just know that my thoughts of Mariah became more infrequent as time passed. My passwords changed to other things. I was able to smile again and just wait on God. The joy of the Lord strengthened me day by day.

Life continued. It was time to bring more closure. My seeking brought me to the conclusion that I wasn't going to get pregnant soon. So, it was time to pack up the nursery. My sweet sister-in-law, Arella, had offered to help. So, I called her and told her I was ready. It was a painful time. We packed in silence, but my sister is a praying woman. I know she was praying down on the inside for my strength. We took down the crib. Every turn of the screwdriver was painful, but we finally got it done. I don't remember much. All I know is that my heart was stored in those boxes, but it brought me one step closer to the closure I needed.

Again, one thing was for sure; I was hearing from God. He had never stopped speaking to me through all of this. I don't even remember when He said it, but I remember just knowing that He was going to bless us with two children. Two more were coming. It was just a matter of when.

One day, as life was moving on, Sister Diane Keesee spoke to me and said, "The Lord is going to give you two children." She said, "I see a boy and a girl. The boy will be very smart, and the girl will have long hair. I don't know which one will come first." I replied to her that I knew. The boy would come first. So, what God had shown me was confirmed. However, when?

As I look back on it now, I see that my focus should not have been on the "when it will happen;" I should have been focused on the walk of getting there.

Oh,, we can't get it twisted! The journey matters. We can't overlook our walk with the Lord during these times. He is on the journey with us. We can't be so overwhelmed that we miss the fellowship with the Lord as He walks us right out of despair and into our promise. The journey of that communion is amazing. It's an unforgettable peace and stillness that you will get that you will forever want to bask in. Don't miss it. Enjoy the journey.

Like Hannah One, I knew it was going to happen. The journey got easier day by day. I praised my way through.

So, know this. As you go through your life's journey,

there will be some rough days, but stay in your position of seeking the Lord. The attacks can be fierce, but God will bring you out, and it will be for His glory. Stand still and see the salvation of God. Stand still and watch how your seeking will bring forth the fruit that you so desire.

As you can see, there were significant people that came into my life just when I needed them. God used them to keep me going. God used them to get me to my next level. Being in those moments, it was sometimes hard to see that God was really working for me, but where I was once blind, now I see. I see the encouragement He sent. I remember the ways that He made, and it has made all the difference.

LET'S PRAY

Oh God, I have found so much comfort from seeking You. Oh, the times of dropping to my knees while carrying a spirit of heaviness[4] have proven to be so beneficial. Oh, the cries to feel the touch from Almighty God has never disappointed. You heard me and delivered me[5] just as Your Word said You would.

So, Father, this is the prayer that I pray for my brothers and sisters. I pray that they too get into the position of seek on a quest to feel Your delivering power. Ah, I pray that they press in to know You in a personal and real way. I pray that their journey becomes a life of communication with You. I pray that You fill them with Your Spirit and bring a life of steadfastness to them.

Oh, Father, I pray that You meet them at the point of their needs. Deliver and set them free. Give them an Isaiah 61 experience. Spirit of the Living God, fall afresh upon them. Give them beauty for ashes. Give them the oil of joy for mourning and a garment of praise for the spirit of heaviness. And we will give You all the glory, and all the honor in Jesus' Name! Amen!

IN MY PRAYER TIME

I was in prayer one day; I could hear the
Spirit of the Lord in me saying,
"The Spirit of the Lord is upon me!"

It was in a beautiful melody that
sounded way off in the distance.

Over and over in my Spirit, I could hear it
as it drew closer and closer.

"The Spirit of the Lord is upon me."

I knew that the Holy Ghost was speaking.
So, I put pen to paper and delivered a message to the
church titled, yes, you guessed it,

"The Spirit of the Lord is upon me."

Oh, that was a beautiful message.
My oldest brother, David, was playing
the guitar that day and he caught on to the melody and
played it each time I would declare it during the message.

"The Spirit of the Lord is upon me."

Don't you realize that your body is the temple of the Holy Spirit, who lives in you and was given to you by God? You do not belong to yourself, for God bought you with a high price. So you must honor God with your body.
1 Corinthians 6:19-20 NLT

So, if the Spirit of the Lord is upon you, the only thing left for you to do is allow Him to keep the house, your house, your temple strong.

CHAPTER SIX
KEEP THE HOUSE STRONG

The Spirit of the Lord is Upon Me

There were promises made by God to both Hannahs. The confirmations had come. We were freed from the bonds that had bound us for so long. We were being healed from our hurts and God was about to reward us for waiting and standing on His promises. I can't help but think of 2 Corinthians 1:20 NIV where it states, "For no matter how many promises God has made, they are 'Yes' in Christ. And so, through Him the 'Amen' is spoken by us to the glory of God."

The only thing the Hannahs had to say was "Amen." That amen meant "it is so." It will happen. Our answer was stamped, sealed, and ready to be delivered. Our faith was going to bring the evidence that God had heard our prayers and answered them. Our faith was bringing what we longed for into fruition.

For Hannah One, her womb was healed. God had

removed the infertility and He positioned her for the birthing process. This time on this year's journey to Shiloh, Hannah One had gotten up a different way. She got up in victory! This time, she got up with an answer!! This time, she got up with joy unspeakable and full of glory. Peninnah was now in that fight to be first by herself. God had answered Hannah's One's request. It was over. He had made her enemies her footstool.

> As 2 Corinthians 2:14 KJV states, "Now thanks be unto God, which always causeth us to triumph in Christ, and maketh manifest the savour of his knowledge by us in every place."

Isn't it wonderful to serve a God that is Himself triumphant? He is victory. Therefore, He totally qualifies to cause us to be just like Him. We are to grab hold of that and expect our breakthrough, knowing that it is coming. It's just a process. Cause means in this case to start something. It's the foundation, the root or origin of a thing. From that, growth or movement comes forth. Then, from that, God's plan reveals itself bit by bit. Before you know it, the triumph has formed and we are all the better for it. What triumph have you asked for? What victory are you waiting to break forth? As an experienced Hannah, let me encourage you to stay the course. Your triumph, His plan, is coming forth.

The Bible says that Hannah One went her way. That means, she got up!!! Imagine the relief she felt. Imagine the confidence she took on. Imagine how thoughts of a new future flooded her mind. Her countenance had changed, and she got up with a pep in her step. Hannah One was able to eat again. She was free.

I remember visiting a church many years ago. My husband and I were probably only friends at the time. A man of God was walking out to the back of the church. I was sitting in the choir stand. He stopped abruptly and out of nowhere, he reached for my hand and simply prayed these words, "Lord, give her her greatest desire." Then, he walked off. Talk about being in the right place at the right time! Oh, my Lord! It's amazing how God had someone pray over my life years before I knew what my greatest desire was. As the years passed, I was like Mary, pondering what he said over and over in my mind. As time moved on, it was evident that having another child was my greatest desire.

As I, Hannah Two, learned how to accept my baby being gone, God was healing me and moving me from that place of hurt. I had been a good person. I felt like I didn't deserve what had happened. I was married. Giving myself to prayer and fasting. Going to church and learning about the Lord. Was this punishment for a past sin? No, of course not. God was simply doing a new thing in me. He was showing me that I was planted for His glory and that from this, regardless of how tragic, how painful, how dark, He would be glorified. Yes, from this suffering, God would be glorified. God blessed us through this so we could be examples of what He could and would do for others. This wasn't just a lesson for the Murphys. This was a lesson for us all. It was a true testament of how the Lord would give me my greatest desire. Approximately a year later, I was with child again. I had no problems with the pregnancy. Although the doctor had me categorized as a high risk, I was getting great reports. When it was close to time to give birth, just to be on the side of caution, they induced my labor. This is when they discovered my baby had hypertachycardia. Hypertachycardia is when the baby's heart is beating faster than normal. In a matter of minutes, we went from going through a normal birthing process that would take hours to an emergency Caesarean section. They prepped me and down the hall we went. Thoughts of the first pregnancy, I am sure, were going through everyone's mind. Were we going to lose this baby too? God forbid. He had prepared me for this. That is why my healing was so important. These moments in time needed me calm. God had given us a promise. We had His Word, His promise, and it was backed up with His yes. We just had to trust the process. I had my promise in view. My thoughts were on me meeting my little one. It was time.

They assured me that everything was going to be all right. Although I didn't feel any pain, I felt them tugging at my body. It wasn't long that I heard the cry of our little one. He was here. They captured a picture of him crying. His eyes were wide open and fixed. I always thought that picture captured the moment when we locked eyes from across the room and he thought, "There is my mommy" and I thought, "There is my baby." Oh, I get chills just thinking about it.

That, of course, was not the end of the story. They had to deal with the hypertachycardia. It was discovered that he had a hole in his heart. God is so AMAZING!!! He had to go from delivery to the neonatal intensive care unit. I, of course, didn't know all of this until later. My family had them wait to tell me because of Mariah. Isn't it wonderful to have a loving and caring family that will protect you? They had admitted me to the hospital, and I was in a room. Finally, one of the OBGYN doctors came in. She said that she didn't know why my family didn't want to tell me what was going on, but my baby was fine. She proceeded to tell me the situation with our baby boy. She said there was nothing to worry about. He would have to take a special medicine twice a day for one year. This will cause the hole in his heart to close. I remember my husband's grandmother standing in the door dancing and giving God praise. What a Mighty God we serve! He had to stay in NICU for some days, but he was fine. The Lord had fulfilled His promise to us. My greatest desire had manifested. I didn't have to go through the same thing again of losing another child. I not only got to fix up the nursery again, I got to use it. He got to wear some of the gender-neutral clothes that had been boxed up. He used the crib. He used to playpen, the bouncer, the highchair, the table and chair set, the car seat, and the special quilts that my aunt had made for Mariah.

God did that!

My God is truly amazing because He blessed Jaylon to be assigned the best cardiologist in Memphis, TN. We administered his meds faithfully every day as prescribed. The Lord blessed us. He was very small for his age because of the meds, but he was healthy. I still remember the last visit to the cardiologist. He showed us this colorful monitor with Jaylon's beating heart. That monitor was beautiful, because that is where he proved to us that the hole had closed. Hallelujah! No more meds. Our baby boy was completely healed. He said that he could live a normal life like any other child. Of course, that still wasn't the end of the story. He was then diagnosed with asthma, but remember Elder Grady Henderson, Jr? He prayed for Jaylon. He told me not to worry, that Jaylon would grow out of the asthma. Sure enough, he did just that. By the time Jaylon got to middle school, he was playing the trombone. No more albuterol. No more breathing machines. No more visits to the emergency room. My son was healed once again. God is faithful.

Oh, my sister, my brother, I speak life over you today. Your story may be totally different from our stories but hurt is still hurt. The Bible says in Malachi 3:11 KJV, "And I will rebuke the devourer for your sakes, and he shall not destroy the fruits of your ground; neither shall your vine cast her fruit before the time in the field, saith the LORD of hosts." Believe it! Some things we will have to go through. So, go through them. What you are going through is your personal journey. Own it! Don't take detours along the way trying to drown your pain in alcohol or numb the pain with other substances. Do what both Hannahs did. We poured out our hearts to a God that does not fail. So, pour your heart out to that same God and expect your promise. Tell Him that you cannot handle it on your own. Trust me, He will walk with you. He will talk with you and He will console you like no one else can. Trust the process. Trust in your God. Psalms 119:71 KJV declares, "It was good for me that I have been afflicted that I might learn thy statutes."

It seems all my life I've heard someone say that our trials come to make us stronger. My life's lessons have taught me that they knew what they were talking about. Going through life teaches us as we go, and we are better for it. We take what we have learned, and we build upon it daily. God orchestrates our steps and moves us through life. It amazes me when I look back at how I have grown in knowing God. Although going through has not been easy, I too can declare, like the Psalmist, that it was good for me that I was afflicted. Synonyms for afflicted are distressed, tormented, aggrieved, stricken, and plagued, but even with such strong words, I can still say that it was good for me. In the Book of Romans, Paul even pondered on his afflictions and sufferings. He concluded in Chapter 8 verse 18 KJV, "For I reckon that the sufferings of this present time are not worthy to be compared with the glory which shall be revealed in us." Paul looked at the bigger picture. He was saying that regardless of what I have to face in this life, it is worth me going through because it can't be compared to the glory and freedom that God will reveal to us. Oh, it is an encouragement to keep going and know that a brighter and a better day is ahead.

That is how you keep the house strong. You are the house. Choose who you hang around. I was always taught to get around the strong saints. Get around folks that can get a prayer through. Get around people that are going somewhere in their faith walk with God. Get around those that will speak life over you. Ask God to lead you to those you need to be around even if it is for a season and not a lifetime. Sometimes, we get that confused and we end up holding on to something or someone longer than needed. The Bible says in Psalm 37:23 KJV that the steps of a good man are ordered by the Lord. Allow Him to order your steps directing your path daily.

When I look back at Hannah One's situation, I see that there was an issue with keeping the house strong. Whether Elkanah, her husband, would admit it or not, he had invited and welcomed division with open arms into his house.

Even today, division is being invited into homes. It comes in all forms. It is not restricted to infidelity and disloyalty to a spouse. Just like committing adultery, inviting substance abuse, gambling habits, pornography, alcoholism, lack of attention, lack of communication, and more, can bring disconnection to the home, the family, and/or the relationship as well. Instead of getting stronger and better with age, there is decline, disfunction, distance, loss, pain, and suffering. Then, if not careful, those same things could possibly lead to devastations like unforgiveness, which further leads from division to broken homes that can never be repaired.

Our decisions matter. Our choices matter. We must be mindful and think things all the way through. Pray about it. Search out the matter, as King Solomon suggested in Proverbs 25. Just because it is customary and it worked for your best friend's cousin's stepfather's uncle does not mean it will work out the same way for you. Division can destroy a home.

Hannah One always had the upper hand. She just didn't realize it. Her upper hand wasn't because Elkanah loved her most, even though many may think that. It was because of her God. Her turning to Him in her time of despair proved Romans 8:31-32 KJV.

"What, then, shall we say in response to these things? If God is for us, who can be against us? He who did not spare his own Son, but gave him up for us all—how will he not also, along with him, graciously give us all things?"

She was a woman of great faith and it was revealed that God a had a divine purpose and plan specifically for her. God used the barrenness of Hannah to restore and bring His temple back into alignment with Him. Think about it. Priest Eli had not kept his own house. At one point in time, the House of Eli was strong, but as his sons Hophni and Phinehas grew up, they changed and started living corrupt and perverse lives. God warned Eli to make the corrections, but he only spoke to them. He did not follow through making the necessary changes to bring his house back into alignment with God. As a result, God removed them. He destroyed their house. Their disobedience led to their demise. His disobedient sons died the very same day. Then when their father heard the news, he died too. Then, upon hearing the news of her husband and father-in-law, Phinehas's wife, Eli's daughter-in-law, gave birth to son. She named him Ichabod meaning the glory has departed. Then, she died.

The old adage "A house divided against itself cannot stand" was very evident in Eli's family and it is still very relevant today. Disobedience divides a home. It tears down the walls and dismantles it brick by brick.

However, moving in obedience to God brings security in Him. Our Lord's intent is to build up, fortify, and protect us not destroy us. That is why obedience in Him is so important. 2 Thessalonians 3:3 NKJV, "But the Lord is faithful, who will establish you and guard you from the evil one." That means that He will insure us. 1 John 3:8b NKJV , "...for the devil has sinned from the beginning. For this purpose, the Son of God was manifested, that He might destroy the works of the devil." So let us always choose God to insure ourselves in God. Choose the right path and walk therein. For it was the desperate desire of a woman that took the way of the Lord, thus insuring herself and turning her captivity. Her end result was an answer to a desperate plea as well as her faith being rewarded with a man child that God would one day use to bring order and peace back to the temple.

LET'S PRAY

Father, Your Word instructs us to walk in the Spirit.[1] *With that comes a confidence in who You are. You are a God of Your Word and You will make good on your promises. You know what is best for us. Your Word declares that Your thoughts are not our thoughts and Your ways are not our ways.*[2] *For as the Heavens are higher than the earth, so are Your ways. You know how to make things work together for our good.*[3] *So, help us, Lord to lean not on our own understanding.*[4] *Help us to trust Your plan and simply say, "Yes, Lord, Your will be done."*

Oh Father, we wait on You. We don't want to get ahead of You. So, help us in the wait. Thy will be done. I pray this prayer in Jesus' Name. Amen.

THE CD TITLED, "A WEALTHY PLACE" BY LASHUN PACE

The Lord used this CD to minister to me. I played it often during my pregnancy. Little did I know how significant it would be the next year as part of my healing journey. As I healed, I leaned heavily on the song on the CD titled, "A Wealthy Place." It carried the promise that God would bring me out into a wealthy place, and I believed it.

> *Psalm 66:12 KJV, "Thou hast caused men to ride over our heads; we went through the fire and through water: but thou broughtest us out into a wealthy place."*

CHAPTER SEVEN
GOD, YOU PROMISED A WEALTHY PLACE

When Hannah One left the temple believing God for a child, the Bible says that the Lord remembered her. The Lord did not forget her request, nor did He forget her vow. She asked Him to look on her affliction. In other words, she was saying to take everything that I have and give me a son [her request] and I will give him back to you [her vow]. I'm sure Hannah One knew the customs of her day that her husband could annul her vow, but this vow was in the will of God. God wanted to use her just as much as she wanted to be used. He remembered her posture and how she approached the throne pouring out her praise to Him and Him alone. Her posture represented more than just her barrenness; it represented all she suffered because of it. God's plan for her was greater than she knew. Her deliverance meant deliverance for God's people. She didn't know it, but God was using it [her deliverance] to bring restoration to His people that were becoming more and more disconnected from Him. It also meant a happier family for her. The Lord looked on everything thing that she had gone through. He took it all into account just like He did for Joseph, who went from being thrown into a pit to being elevated to second in command. Let me not forget Job, who experienced the loss of seemingly everything except his life, but God restored him and He still could testify for him and ask those same words from Job 2:3 KJV, "…have you considered my servant Job?" Each of them received restoration beyond where they started.

Hannah One was finally pregnant. Her season of reaping had finally come, and in due time she and Elkanah were the proud parents of a baby boy. They named him Samuel. God had blessed her, just as she had asked. Now it was time for her to honor her vow and give him back to God as she promised, since Elkanah honored the vow she had made. Many people would have reneged on their vow. However, God strategically chose her for this. Remember, the Bible said that He (God) had shut up her womb. She was one of many women chosen to be an example of righteousness, perseverance, and commitment. She represented her God, and her God honored her for it. She finally had her greatest desire.

Hannah Two prayed over her son as well, and asked the Lord to use him. However, God had promised two children to Hannah Two and after three years, she was with child again. Yes, I was with child again. God did that! This pregnancy, however, proved to be the worst one of all.

Knowing what had happened with Mariah and knowing the prophecy that this child would be a girl, I experienced a lot of torment. The enemy came after me and this baby trying to destroy our destiny. It seems the more I advanced in the pregnancy, the more I was tormented. I had changed to a new doctor and had not shared with her what I was going through until far into the third trimester. On this particular day, I was at a weekly routine visit to the doctor's office. There, she gave me the news that my baby didn't have a lot of amniotic fluid around her, and they needed to induce my labor that day. I then shared more of my story about Mariah with her. We were standing at the time. She told me to sit down, and she grabbed a seat too. She then grabbed my hands and went into prayer. She rebuked the devourer and spoke life over my baby and me. Yes! My doctor was a Christian, and she allowed the Lord to use her that day to help me get to my promise. Can you guess what time of year it was? It was the beginning of the year, and the saints were in their yearly three-day shut-in, with prayer and fasting at the church. I had contacted someone at the church. So, the prayers were going up for me. God was up to something.

I had driven myself to the doctor's office that day. So, I drove on to the hospital blessing my faithful God. My mind was in a good place because the Lord had used my doctor to speak faith, hope, belief, and trust in our Almighty God. This outcome was going to be different. I had called my husband to leave work and he came right on. Once again, we were taking this journey together. They hooked me up to the sonogram and this time, the monitor was different. There was her little heart beating normally. She was moving and breathing and doing just what she needed to do. This season was similar, but the outcome was different. Remember the commercial with the camel that goes around asking what day is it? Well, in the words of Mr. Camel, "Guess what day it is." No, not hump day. It is the same month and day that my Mariah was stillborn, and I shared that with my doctor. God was truly up to something. Would my baby girl, my gift from God, be born on the same day as Mariah's stillborn date?

They induced my labor some time that day but slowed down the process. Why? My doctor wanted me to give birth the next day. I expressed my concern and told her that I felt the Lord was in the plan and wanted it to be the same day. She refused, thinking it was best for this baby's birthday to be on a different date. So, I had a bouncing baby girl the next morning. God had fulfilled His promise to me.

For many years, I had wished she had honored my wishes. As I said before, being pregnant with my second baby girl after the loss of my first baby girl was so difficult. So, I thought that having their dates on the same day would be how God would complete His promise to us. Despite the torment, despite the fear, God was showing me that this time would be different. With all the noise that the enemy wanted me to focus on, God was reassuring me every single day that this baby would live and not die. By then, I was a different woman. I was more equipped to deal with the situations at hand. I was stronger, and just needed to use my weapons and my words against the attacks of my enemies. Although them having the same birth date would have been so cool and sentimental, I view it another way now. Mariah's date was like my night, but Kristyn's date was my dawning of a new day, my morning. The saying, "Weeping may endure for a night, but joy comes in the morning" took on new meaning. Kristyn was born in the morning, and she brought us great joy. She brought a new day, for real. I thank God for the journey and that He walked with me. It reminds me of that small portion of scripture with the huge meaning in Hebrews 13:5b NLT where it says, "Never will I leave you. Never will I forsake you." He is with us!

1 The Lord is my shepherd; I shall not want.

2 He maketh me to lie down in green pastures: he leadeth me beside the still waters.

3 He restoreth my soul: he leadeth me in the paths of Righteousness for his name's sake.

4 Yea, though I walk through the valley of the shadow of death, I will fear no evil: for thou art with me; thy rod and thy staff they comfort me.

5 Thou preparest a table before me in the presence of mine enemies: thou anointest my head with oil; my cup runneth over.

6 Surely goodness and mercy shall follow me all the days of my life: and I will dwell in the house of the Lord for ever.

Psalm 23:1-6 KJV

Oh, when I think how I could have allowed the noise and the fear of what could have happened consume me, I rejoice. For God gave me a beautiful testimony. He kept His promise. He proved Himself to be my Shepherd. I am able to say that He was Psalm 23 to me. When I've shared my testimony, people have been amazed at how God has brought me through with overwhelming victory. They immediately feel sympathy and want to say "I am so sorry." Back then, those words were a comfort to me, but today, I am healed. I can share it now as a testimony to say, if He did it for me, He will do it for you. For I know that He meant it for my good. Truly, all things work together for the good of them that love the Lord. He changed our sad and melancholy days to laughter and joy.

The scripture in Psalm 66:10-12 KJV says, "For thou, O God, hast proved us: Thou hast tried us, as silver is tried. Thou broughtest us into the net; Thou laidst affliction upon our loins. Thou hast caused men to ride over our heads; We went through fire and through water: But thou broughtest us out into a wealthy place."

As I listen to the song, "A Wealthy Place" [1] now, it is bittersweet. It brings back a flood of memories and emotions, but I thank my God I grew from the experience. At that time, I was playing that song over and over as I strived to get to my place of abundance. I was seeking in tears with a bleeding heart. Oh, but I am so happy to announce that my striving was not in vain. I found healing. The Spirit of the Lord kept me. The Spirit of the Lord sustained me. The Spirit of the Lord was upon me, and He guided me right into my Wealthy Place.

I believe God was intentional in the entire process. Like Hannah One, I was chosen for this. From the preacher stopping in his tracks to grab my hand and pray that God grant me by greatest desire, to the song that Lashun Pace released, God was intentional. I must say it again. It really proves that all things work together for the good of them that love the Lord.

When I say all things work together, I don't just mean the circumstances of life. All things also include our works. We know God is going to do His part, but remember we have our part to do as well. When we work in obedience and in harmony with God, whether in prayer or some other action, we will see the fruit of our labor.

I think the story of Ruth is a prime example of that. After a long journey of heartache, God brought Ruth and Naomi into His favor. Their path led them straight to their Wealthy Place. I also look at Joseph, his journey was apart from his family. He experienced jealousy, slavery, lies, and prison but even in the midst of all that, God was teaching him leadership, endurance, and faithfulness. He too was brought into his Wealthy Place. Oh, let me not forget Peter. Even after denying Jesus, his repentance and forgiveness brought him to a place of abundance as he preached to three thousand about the love of Jesus Christ.

Remember Ziglag? David and his men had lost everything, but they couldn't remain in that melancholy state because God had said, "Go and you shall recover all."[2] God not only gave them victory over their enemy, but He gave them victory when they went to recover their families and possessions. They even took the spoil of their enemies. The Lord blessed them overwhelmingly.

Whether on the mountaintop or in the lowest valley, I shout it for all to hear: God will bring you out into a wealthy place. Strive to get there. Trust God's process. Trust His plan and wait on the manifestation of His promise. I've heard the Lord say these words to me several times, "I'll show you." In other words, He was saying I will prove what I promised. He has not failed me yet. I am in my wealthy place.

LET'S PRAY

God, You did that! You proved that You are not a man that You should lie.³ God, You kept Your Word. You promised not only me, but You promised us a wealthy place and You made good on Your promise. Thank You! Thank You so much for meeting me at the point of my need. Oh God! How I bless You! I honor You! You are my God.

Now Lord, look on these Your people and all that concerns them. They need You. Breathe on them. Restore unto them that which has been stolen. Restore unto them that which has been broken. Restore, my God, unto them that which has been lost. Restore unto them that which has been bound. Do it, Lord! Bring every high place down. Bring every low place up! Give them to speak to those mountains. Move them out of their way. Let their wealthy places come forth. We already know that You can and believe that You will. You will make good on Your promises. We claim it by faith. It's in Jesus' Name that I pray. Amen!

PROPHECY RECEIVED IN JULY 2021

"I see the Lord taking you back 25 years."

Wait! What? What does that mean? At the time, I didn't have a clue what Prophetess Tmeiko Dowell was talking about. It had not come to me that my baby would have been 25 years old that next January. So, once again, I did as Mary, the mother of Jesus did, I pondered what she said in my heart.

Then, some months later, it came to me as the Lord began to deal with me about the number 25, that it represents redemption (twenty) and grace (five). Those two meanings combined have provided the consistency I needed to survive. I needed something to hold on to. They showed up even when I didn't want to show up. I didn't realize it, but I needed them to help me become the woman of God that He created me to be. God wanted to use me to bring Him glory. He wanted me to be a tree of righteousness just like the Word of God declares in Isaiah 61:3 KJV.

To appoint unto them that mourn in Zion, to give unto them beauty for ashes, the oil of joy for mourning, the garment of praise for the spirit of heaviness; that they might be called trees of righteousness, the planting of the Lord, that he might be glorified.

Going back twenty-five years helped me to see how I have grown in faith. Even before I gave my life to Christ, there is still no doubt that it has been Him all along Who has qualified me for anything I set out to do. He gave me what I needed most so that I could bring glory to Him. Therefore, I have enough humility in me to know that I could not have made it without Him. He has given me hope and I thank Him for it. He deserves my glory.

Little did I know that everything I had learned from my own journey would be needed for this next battle. As a matter of fact, I believe He developed and prepared me to be ready for this one. There was a third Hannah that showed up in my life and she needed a new start as well. It hit fast and it hit hard, but I was not going down without a fight. I HAD to declare, to decree, to proclaim and to command over my third Hannah these words, "You shall live and not die and declare the works of the Lord. You shall have A NEW BEGINNING in Christ!!"

CHAPTER EIGHT
A NEW BEGINNING

Time to Stand Up
By Kristyn Murphy

At a certain point in our lives, I believe we get too comfortable with our circumstances. We fail to remember things can change in an instant, and the state of comfort that we knew for so long will no longer be. This happened to me. For as long as I can remember, I was happy and bubbly. I had always kind of lived in my own world. But as the years went by and I got older, I began to see parts of the world that I was unfamiliar with. There was so much about this world and the people living in it that I didn't know or understand. I was not fully prepared for the hurt, confusion, peer pressure, and overall chaos that I had experienced during my teenage years. This was my first new beginning. The thing to remember about new beginnings is that not every new beginning will bring you what you want, but it will bring you what you need.

As a child, I taught myself how to cope with things by

suppressing my feelings. So, by the time I arrived at this new point in my journey and was faced with all this chaos, I considered myself a pro at bottling up my feelings. As time went on, I got to a certain point where I looked up and that happy and bubbly girl that I had always known myself to be was now unrecognizable. I was lost. I had internalized all the things done and said to and about me, and now I believed them. I believed that I wasn't enough. I believed that I didn't deserve a voice. I believed that I lacked what it took to succeed. The devil planted those seeds, and slowly they began to grow within me. I remember coming home from school one day. I walked home from the bus stop, and as soon as I walked through the door, I let out a huge sigh of relief. That was the moment of my day where I could finally breathe.

My normal routine when I got home from school was to pace around downstairs and vent about what I was going through before anyone got home. I would do this for hours, just venting to God. One particular day after walking through the door and releasing my sigh, I went upstairs to pace. I started talking to God as I normally would and I began to tell Him about how I was giving up. I was vulnerable to all the negative thoughts that the devil was planting in my mind - including the suicidal ones. I was broken. I was tired. I missed the happy and bubbly me. No one was home, so I was screaming, crying, and trying to get God to see me because I felt so alone. I just didn't understand why I was going through what I was going through, but I don't think it was meant for me to understand. All I needed to know was that it wasn't the end for me.

Fast forward, I graduated high school and began college. I was still carrying those emotions with me and mentally, I was getting worse. I was allowing the enemy to win the war that was going on in my mind. I was praying and asking for God's help, but it felt like He had forgotten about me. I was stuck in a deep, dark hole, and I couldn't find my way out. I remember getting out of my bed one night with my mind made up to throw in the towel. I remember vividly going to find a pharmacy bag in the pantry holding inside a new bottle of medicine. I turned around and as soon as I made my first step forward to go up to my room, I heard "No." It was silent and firm, yet very gentle. I stopped in my tracks and thought for a second. I had never really heard God before and I questioned whether it was Him. I believe it was, because after hearing the response, I didn't feel scared, I felt safe. The "No" that He said to me was a short response, yet it was filled with so much meaning. The "No" meant that there was far more in store for me. I know God was saying to me, "Don't give up on Me. I see you. I hear you. I am working on your behalf. I need you to trust Me." I put the medicine back and decided that it was time to ask for help. I talked with my parents and brother about what I was experiencing. They proved to me that I was not alone. They were right there praying, advising, and just being what I needed. I didn't have to walk the journey alone. I started trying to pray more consistently and improve my relationship with God overall, but it was still hard for me to drown out the evil voices in my head.

This journey was not a short one. It was a long journey that consisted of both highs and lows. Sometimes, I would get discouraged and frustrated because it felt like I was taking one step forward and fifteen steps back, or stuck in a cycle. I was exhausted, but I kept going.

The conversation came up about me moving away for college. As parents having a daughter who is experiencing such a hard season of her life, they questioned whether I would be able to make it on my own. I, myself, even questioned whether I would be okay or not. I pondered about moving for a while. I imagined how things might change for me, and I prayed about it. Then, finally, one day I went downstairs to my mom's office and sat on her couch. I looked her straight in the eye and told her, "Mama, you have to let me go." She expressed her concerns to me and told me that she and my dad would talk about it.

Time passed and I was packing my room to move three hours away to survive in a new city alone. The risk was so great. I would lose a lot, but I knew it was necessary. This leap of faith was my chance to isolate and figure things out. It was a chance for me to find that happy and bubbly girl again. It was another new beginning. But, again, a new beginning does not mean that everything was about to come easy and smooth. Sometimes, things get harder before they get better.

A NEW BEGINNING

My relationship with Christ grew day by day. And, I will be honest, it was not easy. Some days, I had nothing to say. Some days, I felt like what I had to say didn't matter because God was tired of me and my cycle of highs and lows. He wasn't. He understands that this life we live isn't easy. He understands and He loves you. In order for me to really understand that, though, my perspective had to change and I had to let a lot of things go. So, you have to try and do the same because it won't just help you with your current storm, but with all of the storms that you have ahead as well.

During my storm, my mom told me about how she saw me in the spirit. I was crunched down on the ground. She said that God told her to tell me to stand up. And, currently, as I am sitting in my bed writing this chapter as a college graduate, still three hours away, living on an answered prayer, I can tell you that eventually, I stood up. Did the storms stop coming? No. Did the depression and anxiety I was experiencing go away? No. But did things start getting better for me? Yes. Why? Because I don't allow the negative voices to take the happy and bubbly girl that I am. I pray. I do things that make me happy. I continue to stand up. Whenever the enemy tries to get me to be crunched down like I was before, I stand firm. So, today, I am telling you to STAND UP. Both Hannahs stood up. I stood up. And I believe in my heart that you can do it too. Your story may be nothing like mine, but whatever you are going through that is causing you to be crunched down like I was, you have to stand up! Every day you have to choose to stand up. The amazing thing about God is that even on the days that you can't, He will meet you exactly where you are. He sees you. He loves you. He has not forgotten about you.

Once you stand up, you will begin to walk again. Walk with God. The more you walk and talk with Him, the more you will hear Him talking back. He will give you understanding, and He will also give you peace and comfort. You will get to another new beginning and realize the assignment was always bigger than you. You have a purpose on this earth. You are meant to be here. You are valuable. The assignment was bigger than both Hannahs, my assignment was bigger than me, and your assignment IS bigger than you. We are not our circumstances. We are not what the enemy tries to tell us we are. We are the children of the Alpha and Omega! So, stand up, stand firm, and remember that you are NEVER alone.

PRAY WITH KRISTYN

Dear Heavenly Father,

First, we want to thank You for the life You have given us. We want to thank You for working behind the scenes for us. Father, right now we are confused, we are broken, we are hurting, and feeling so many emotions that we do not understand. But God, we know that You are capable of turning our confusion into understanding, our brokenness into wholeness, and giving us peace and comfort to replace all the other emotions that the enemy is trying to put into our lives. Father, we come to You for Your help because we know that You are the only one that can take our problems and turn them around for our good. Bless us, Lord; give us the things we need and the desires of our hearts. You are an All-knowing God, so give us the strength to accept and let go of the things that You know are not meant for us. Today, we are giving all our situations to You. We understand now, Lord, that we can't fix it by ourselves. We can't depend on self. So, Father, we are trusting You 100% to work in our lives. We love You, God.

In Jesus' name we pray.

Amen.

SWIM TO THE TOP!!!

Several years ago, I dreamed that I was in the depths of the ocean. The dream started at that point. It was a dark place. I don't know how I got there or if I was trying to figure a way out or even if I wanted to get out. I was just there. After seeing myself in that state, I saw a bright light approaching me from my left. The light lit up the waters. I remember the blueness of the water. From the light came a voice that said, "Swim to the top." In the depths of the ocean, I took a deep breath knowing that on that one breath I would have to make it to the top. I then began to swim up. Stroke after stroke, I went higher and higher. Finally, I made it. When I came up out of the water, I was in an area where many people were sitting all around. It was so bright and sunny. It was similar to a Sea World setting where we would go to see the whales perform. Everyone was happy to see me make it. I didn't know everyone. It was as if I was the center of attention and the main attraction. My husband was there, kneeling with his hand extended to help me out of the water, saying, "I didn't think you would make it back this time." Back this time?! Apparently, I had been in this dark place before. Now, when I think on this dream, I see that it revealed to me that I had a future and a hope. It revealed that there was more to my story. God did not want me to remain in that dark place of hopelessness and despair. He wanted me to swim to the top and see the salvation, the brightness of God. He wanted me to see my future. He wanted me to Get Up! It was time to live.

CHAPTER NINE
HANNAH, GET UP

We All Are Hannah

Although I did not want it. I understand it now. It is 25+ years later. Looking back, I am so thankful for everyone God used on my journey. They had what I needed. The Lord used them as well as dreams and visions to help me understand where He wanted to take me.

The Bible says that we are salt of the earth. I understand now, as I am sure those older mothers did whom I surrounded myself with as a "baby saint." I understand that I cannot lose my savor. The trials, the things I go through, come to enhance my savor. They are like a supplement needed to develop and position me where God desires for me to be. My trials came to make a stronger servant of the Most High, and a better wife, mother, daughter, sister, auntie, cousin, and friend.

Though, I sobbed telling my story, I rejoice to know that someone will be delivered in some way because of it. I refuse to believe that I went through all that to keep silent. The more I write, the more reasons I see why I needed to endure to the end and finish this book. That is why I said you have to enjoy the journey. Every chapter of your life develops into your book of life. Live your life to the best of your ability. Allow God to mold and develop you into what He wants you to be, joining the many that are also called Hannah, for if we really look at it, we all are Hannah in some form or fashion. So, don't take the role of the Potter. That's not your job. We are not to conform to our own ways nor the ways of this world. As the Potter makes us, He is not making us just for ourselves. He is molding us to bless others. He is molding us to birth out others. He is molding us to encourage others. It could very well be that you are Hannah to pray others through. You as Hannah could be representing your family, your church, your job, your friend, your community, or even a nation. Prepare yourself to represent well.

I consider life for me during that time as a great suffering, but God was developing me and giving me "every part" like He told me He wanted to. However, receiving each part would be up to me. How deep did I want to go in Him? How high did I want to go in Him? Was I willing to move past the fear and say, "Forget it, I am just going to do it and deal with what I have to face when I have to face it." Fear of the unknown has talked so many people out of taking a leap of faith. Even in writing this book, I have had so many emotions, but I keep telling myself ~ die empty. Don't take this book to the grave. So, I decided to say, with surrendered hands, okay God, bring it on. Give me every part of Your plan for me. So, step by step, God has been building a little girl that sat on the ground to make mud pies into a woman of faith and steadfastness in Him. My willingness to surrender is the reason why He gave me this part to play. He gave this role to put pen to paper and hopefully and prayerfully change someone's mind on giving up and throwing in the towel. Reminding them to remember the promises that God spoke over them and advising them to take that step towards liberty in Christ. Being that cheerleader to say, "You can do it. You don't have to stay there!"

Prayers like Hannah's are not just for our own personal situations. Those prayers are teachers that show us how to pray for others. When I receive prayer requests now, I think, what if this was me or my family member or my best friend? Those prayers teach us empathy, whereby we are able to move from our own personal situations and petition Heaven on behalf of others. All we need to be is sincere and willing to pray for the sake of someone else, whether you know what is going on with that individual or not.

True story: earlier this year, one Saturday around 3 a.m., the Holy Spirit said, "Get up and pray." He didn't say why. I started drifting off back to sleep. He said, "You would want someone to do it for you." I then jumped right up not knowing any details. I began to just walk and pray as the Spirit of the Lord led. I prayed so until it felt like angels were in the house with me. After I finished, I got back in bed. During the prayer, the Lord never revealed why I was praying. He just allowed the persons to walk through the door about three hours later. Their story was horrific, but their outcome was victory. When they shared what they had been through and the timing of it all, I knew God had me up for them. I'm so glad I got up and took it personally. It was another Hannah victory.

So, to all the Hannahs out there, I ask. What is God calling you to? What or who keeps tugging at your heart? Pray them through. Is it the government? Is it the youth, the homeless, battered women, wounded veterans? Whatever or whomever God is calling you to represent, go boldly to the throne of grace. Get a good grip on the horns of the altar and pray through. Praying through is praying until you are convinced that God has not only heard but has answered. It is knowing down on the inside that He is on the case. Even if you don't receive the answer that you were praying for, stay the course. The answer that God gives is the answer that is needed. Every piece of a puzzle is not shaped the same. Some look weird. Some look like they don't belong, but they are all needed to form the big picture. My advice to you is to add the pieces regardless of how they look. In the end, you will see your masterpiece. You can then say it was worth it. That's growth.

I know God has called me to write this book. I know God has called me to pray. Am I perfect? I absolutely am not, which is why it took me so long to write this. I had to just say to myself, "Better to write it and they not like what they read than to not write it and they never get the chance to read it." There was so much more to the stories of the two Hannahs getting up than being barren and losing a baby. These were just the routes God took to continue them on their journeys of getting up.

About three years ago, my husband was going through a situation. It looked bad. We both were believing God. Every morning, I was obeying the Lord, laying prostrate before Him in prayer crying out for help. I was praying not only for our situation but for the others. Guess what happened? Things got worse before they got better. I kept praying, laid out before the Lord. During this time, the Lord was showing me things in the Spirit. I was maturing spiritually. He was working on me. Many days passed. Things kept getting worse. I then felt led to get some help in prayer. My husband gave me permission to ask about six people to help us pray. My husband was praying. I was praying. Others were praying. As for me, I honestly cannot tell you how many mornings I lay on that floor praying. I would say it was about forty days. Then it happened. One morning after praying, I heard the Holy Spirit speak to my spirit and say, "You don't have to pray about that anymore." I knew that the answer had been released. I knew God had worked that situation out. It just hadn't manifested, but later that day, my husband called me on his lunch break and said, and I paraphrase, "It is over." God had worked on his behalf and gave him the victory. That it how I prayed through.

That is how I waited on God to deliver and deliver He did. For those forty days of prayer, it wasn't just about our situation; I was drowning out the noise of our situation by praying for others and blessing God. I was drawing closer to God and learning His ways.

Hannah One had Eli the priest to speak to her, but this time I, Hannah Two, had the Holy Ghost speak to me and say, "You don't' have to pray about that anymore." In other words, the Spirit of the Lord was saying to me, "I have heard your petition. I have heard your prayer and I have answered in your favor. Hannah, get up!"

Oh, my friends, as this message developed over the years at various churches and just from life, the story revealed that we are all Hannah in one way or another. We all face situations in our lives that can challenge our core, that challenge our purpose, that even challenge our commitment to God. Just like Hannah One went through the process, all Hannahs have to go through their process with a made-up mind that this great affliction that has come upon them will not take them out. All Hannahs, and that includes you, me, our cousin, our co-workers, our pastor's wife, the next-door neighbor, the mayor, the homeless woman downtown, the manager at the grocery store, the president of the university, our most favorite teacher from elementary school, and every mail carrier. We all are Hannahs – male or female. We all go through, but not just that; how we go through matters too.

1. It matters how we prepare before the devastation comes.

2. It matters how we journey through it day after day.

3. It matters how we come out. Are we the same as we were when we went in? Are we better or are we worse?

As for me, I didn't know exactly where God was taking me, I just knew I wanted to go. I trusted Him enough that I would come out with victory. I mean, after all, the fight is fixed. WE WIN!!! So, why not trust the process, God's Way?

Again, Psalm 119:71-72 KJV states, "It is good for me that I have been afflicted; that I might learn thy statues. The law from Your mouth is more precious to me than thousands of pieces of gold and silver."

Being barren, the loss of a baby, or any type of suffering does not feel good. So, why would the Psalmist associate affliction with goodness? It is because the goodness comes after the affliction. It wasn't that the affliction itself was good but where it took you, where you ended up, how you looked when you came up, that is what was good.

In our preparation time, we should follow Colossians 3:1-2 KJV.

"If ye then be risen with Christ, seek those things which are above, where Christ sitteth on the right hand of God.

Set your affection on things above, not on things on the earth."

This scripture admonishes us as believers to seek for and set our gaze on the things of God. After all, He IS God, you know. What He has to offer us is far greater than anything this world could offer. So Hannahs, do as Matthew 6:19-21 KJV says,

> *Lay not up for yourselves treasures upon earth, where moth and rust doth corrupt, and where thieves break through and steal: But lay up for yourselves treasures in heaven, where neither moth nor rust doth corrupt, and where thieves do not break through nor steal: For where your treasure is, there will your heart be also.*

Over twenty years ago, I was at the church I attended, praying. It was probably at one of those third Saturday prayer gatherings. As I was on my knees in deep prayer, I saw a vision of a girl in a fetal position. I couldn't see her face. I just knew she needed help. All types of thoughts came to mind as to who this young lady was. Was she my future daughter? Was she my niece or a cousin? Was she my co-worker? Was she a young lady in my future or was she me? All these many years later, I have pondered on who she was. I have since concluded that she was all of us. She was Hannah. At some point in our lives, we all become Hannah regardless of our physical position, wealth or poverty, multiple degrees or a high school education, saved or declaring that "God is still working on me." Regardless of our status, We Are All Hannah!

It has been my utmost prayer to help someone to get up from that state of melancholy, defying the odds that are stacked against them, and drive forward with every ounce of energy they have in them. That vision really was my future daughter, but was also my husband, my son, my parents, my brothers, my cousin, and so many others. I've heard many people say, if you mess with mine, I'll fight. Well, let it be known, I'll fight too, but my fight is not physical. My fight is spiritual, and it moves mountains.

In my introduction I said, "Hear me, my friends, what the Spirit is saying to you through me today." Today, I speak to you and say, "Hannah, Get Up."

LET'S PRAY

Lord, we want to get up after such great afflictions. Your Word declares that many are the afflictions of the righteous, but the Lord delivers them out of them all.[1] Father, help us to get to our deliverance. Father, help us to get to our breakthroughs and be triumphant just as Your Word declares. Help us to rest in You even when we can't see our way. Help us to abide in Your Presence even the more. It gets rough sometimes. The load some days is almost unbearable, but help us to stay in Your Word to gain encouragement. Give us who we can talk to. Put the right people in our path. Help us on our journeys and continue to remind us that it gets better. This too shall pass. In Jesus' Name I pray. Amen.

"Look straight ahead, and fix your eyes on what lies before you. Mark out a straight path for your feet; stay on the safe path."
Proverbs 4:25-26 NLT

I was watching a movie with my husband one day called *Land*.[1] It was a story of a woman named Edee whose life was abruptly altered by the sudden tragic death of her husband and son. In this movie, she disconnected herself from the world and moved away to live as a hermit on what looked like a secluded mountain. In this new life, she found that she was not prepared to endure the harsh conditions that isolation on this mountain would bring. She soon found herself in a predicament that would put an end to her misery and pain. Although it was a hard way to die, it seemed welcomed. In what seemed to be her final moments, as death drew near due to starvation, a lone hunter found her almost lifeless. With the assistance of the doctor and the grace of God, they were able to nurse her back to health. Once alert, she asked the hunter, "How did you find me?"

He responded, "You were in my path."

My husband looked at me and said, "That will preach!"

In the verses above, Solomon advises us to be watchful and follow straight on the set path. We are to set our sights on that path and conduct ourselves orderly and cautiously as we walk it out. We always say that the steps of a good man are ordered by the Lord. Well, the hunter was the good man in this story, whether she wanted him to be or not. God led him to her, and He leads us as well, if we allow Him to. That path will not only lead us to our answered prayers, but it will allow us to be the answer to the prayers of others. God will use us to help others. It is on our individual paths that we will be able to say these words to someone in need, "You were in my path."

CHAPTER TEN

YOU WERE IN MY PATH

Edee's life journey dished out very hard blows. They were so hard she lost her will to live. She felt helpless and hopeless. Her harsh reality was she didn't want to feel anymore. She wanted the noise in her head gone. She wanted the memories to cease. She didn't want the constant reminders of her husband and son. There was a huge hollowness in her heart. Her sister couldn't fill it. The therapist couldn't bring her closure. Even her own solution couldn't rid her of her pain.

How many times have you tried to be like Harry Houdini, the great magician that was a master at escaping difficult situations? How many times have you thought that you would be better off dead? What saved you? What caused you to keep putting one foot in front of the other despite the pain to even think of moving forward?

What caused the woman with the issue of blood to get in the press to touch the hem of Jesus' garment even though she was full of disappointments and was broken in various ways? What made the centurion soldier tell Jesus, "Just speak the Word and my son will be healed"? What caused the blind man to keep screaming, "Jesus, Son of David, have mercy on me" despite others telling him to be quiet? What made the thief on the cross look towards Jesus and say to Him, "Remember me when You come into Your Kingdom"?

Jesus was in their path and through Him, hope was in their path. Remember the woman at the well. Jesus had told His disciples, "I must needs go through Samaria." Jesus orchestrated a path for them. Each and every one of them were in His path on purpose, and you know what? We are in His path too. Proverbs 16:9 NKJV states, "A man's heart plans his way: but the Lord directs his steps." Somehow, we end up in the right place to meet Jesus. Whether it is like the woman at a well that went at a chosen time to draw water or like Saul on the way to Damascus with the intent to destroy the saints of God, Jesus was in their path. That meeting would change their lives for good. You know why? They were willing to yield and accept it.

There are many that have testified that Jesus was in their path. He may have used someone else to be His hands and His feet, but it was Him. He may have chosen an ordinary person to be His voice and speak life to someone's dead situation, but it was still Him. The Bible says in Psalm 107:20 KJV, "He sent His Word, and healed them, and delivered them from their destructions."

When I look at my life way back as far as even kindergarten, my little five-year-old best friend, Genia from church, comforted me on the first day of school and said, "Marilyn, it will be okay." My life changed that day. God put my best friend in my path to comfort me.

I even think back to when I was traveling out of the country. We made it to the hotel. I was on the right floor to get to my room but I could not find it. Fear set in. I panicked at 2 in the morning. There was a phone on a table. I picked it up, stating in a frantic voice who I was and that I couldn't find my room. A voice came on but I could barely hear it. It sounded muffled and in a different language, but I still explained my situation and hung up the phone with hope that someone understood what I was saying even though I couldn't understand them. I stood there. I know I could have gotten on the elevator but there was one problem. I had a fear of getting on elevators alone. So, there I was, halfway around the world, and I was in one of the worst predicaments of my life, so I thought. All of a sudden, the elevator doors opened. It was a white gentleman being escorted to his room by a bellman. The bellman asked me if everything was okay. By this time, I was not good, but seeing them, I started to calm down. I am sure they both saw it. I told him that I couldn't find my room. He said, "Oh, no worries. I will help you." He said, "Let me get him settled and then I will assist you." Oh my God! Was this just a coincidence or was the white gentleman an angel? Where did he come from? To this day, I don't know. However, if

I ever met him again, he would be able to say to me, "You were in my path." Maybe it was just a coincidence, but to and for me, he was my angel. Although he assisted me indirectly, it was because of him the bellman came to the floor in the first place. Actually, the bellman could say the same thing, "Oh, no worries, you were in my path."

I know God was in the midst of that situation. I needed Him to be. The bellman took me down the hall through another area to get to my room. As we walked, I thought to myself, there was no way in this world I would have taken this path alone. It was like I went to another building. When we got to the room, he showed me around and how to work the lights with my door card. I am so thankful I was in the bellman's path. God used him to get me to my next. He allowed him to walk me right to it.. Oh, I am so glad Jesus does not judge us for our phobias. He just makes sure He is right there to help us work through them. He meets us at the point of our needs.

I have since learned to conquer my fear of elevators. I mean, I serve the God of all flesh, the God of all peace, the God of all comfort. Surely, He is the God of all elevators. Now, I step on elevators with confidence, knowing that I have the power and authority of Jesus Christ to command each of them to take me where I need to go with no issues.

Hannah One was on the path of Priest Eli, but not only him. I believe she was in Peninnah's path as well. Peninnah drove her to her lowest point to get to her miracle. Then, there was me. I was on the path of several others that would minister and prophesy to me to get me to praise God where I was so that in due season God would answer my prayers. My journey has brought such stability to my life. I am now a strong prayer warrior. God has developed me to stand on the battlefield not only for myself but for others. I pray and go to battle. I pray and ask questions later, if any need to be asked. God has opened doors where I pray with and for people across the country. God now uses me to get in the path of others.

Finally, there is you. Where are you? What is going on in your life? What do you need from the Lord? Whatever your request is, remember that you need to be in the right place with the right posture to get to your answer. Look at the different lives of people around you. Look at different people in the Bible. Read the journeys of others. See how they got where they needed to be. Remember, we are all Hannah. We must walk out our destinies. Just know that God will put you on the right path to get the help you need. So, let me do what I feel I was called to do right now. Let me admonish whoever you are to do as so many have done before you. Join the fight. Join the best "Me Too" movement that has ever crossed borders and boundaries, countries and continents. Join the "Me Too" movement that has taken the story of Hannah in the Bible and said, "That can be me. I can get up! I will get up! I must get up! I am up." Allow me to whisper to you like a still small voice. Allow me to yell it if I need to. Allow me to admonish you today. Get

Up! It's time. For out of your pain shall come forth a new mindset, a new you.

"[Insert Your Name Here], GET UP and do what the Lord says do. Obey God!!!"

LET'S PRAY

Lord, I have done what You placed in my heart to do. I have testified of Your goodness. It is now my prayer that others are able to grab this message of hope and run with it. It is my prayer that they are able to overcome every obstacle that is placed before them and become the vessel that You have called them to be. It is my prayer that You bless them indeed. [2] Meet them at the point of their needs, deliver them, and set them free. As you said in the Book of Luke to Simon Peter, "Simon, Simon, Satan hath desired to have you, that he may sift you as wheat, but I have prayed for thee that thy faith fail not..." [3] Oh, thank You, Jesus! Thank You for praying not only for Simon Peter, but thank You, Jesus, for praying for us all. Thank You for allowing us all to be on Your path. Thank You for praying for the reader of this book. It is indeed my prayer that he or she is able to get up and get moving. I rebuke the devourer. I rebuke the devil right now in the Name of Jesus. Satan, take your hands off God's property. We belong to God. Therefore, we declare that no weapon that is formed against us shall prosper. [4] We have a heritage from the Lord. We have the victory, overwhelming victory, and we chose to be free in Jesus, for whom the Son sets free is free indeed. [5]

*It is in Jesus' Name that we pray,
thank God, AMEN!*

HANNAH, GET UP!
THE END

ENDNOTES

LETTER FROM THE AUTHOR
1. Romans 8:1

INTRODUCTION
1. Varsity Company International. (1997). Barren. In *Illustrated Dictionary of the Bible* (Nelson's Super Value Series, p.136).

CHAPTER ONE: TWO HANNAHS
1. Walker, Hezekiah. "Second Chance." YouTube.
2. Hezekiah Walker - Second Chance (youtube.com)
3. Stevens, Ray. "Everything is Beautiful." The Music Box Company 3090 https://themusicboxcompany.com/product/everything-is-beautiful/
4. Genesis 37:3

CHAPTER FOUR: DROWN OUT THE NOISE
1. Psalm 27:11
2. Psalm 119:105

CHAPTER FIVE: INTO THE POSITION OF SEEK
1. Psalm 96:9

2. Psalm 66:2

3. Pace, LaShun. "A Wealthy Place." A Wealthy Place. Savoy Records, 1996. CD.

4. Isaiah 61:3

5. Psalm 34:4

CHAPTER SIX: KEEP THE HOUSE STRONG

1. Galatians 5:16

2. Isaiah 55:8 KJV

3. Romans 8:28

4. Proverbs 3:5

CHAPTER SEVEN: GOD, YOU PROMISED A WEALTHY PLACE

1. Pace, LaShun. "A Wealthy Place." YouTube. 3115

2. https://www.youtube.com/watch?v=DhpAnLdTam8

3. I Samuel 30:8

4. Numbers 23:19

CHAPTER NINE: HANNAH, GET UP

1. Psalm 34:19

CHAPTER TEN: YOU WERE IN MY PATH

1. Wright, R. (Director). (2021). *Land* [Film]. Focus Features LLC
2. I Chronicles 4:10
3. Luke 22:31-32a
4. Isaiah 54:17
5. John 8:36

Milton Keynes UK
Ingram Content Group UK Ltd.
UKHW022250051124
450708UK00014B/1058